FA...

WEDDING
SPEECHES
AND
TOASTS

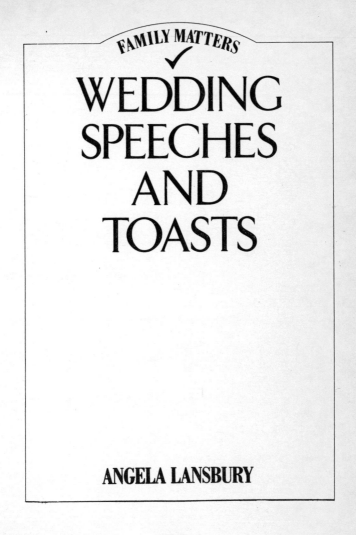

FAMILY MATTERS

WEDDING SPEECHES AND TOASTS

ANGELA LANSBURY

WARD LOCK

© Text Ward Lock Limited 1988
© Illustrations Ward Lock Limited 1988

First published in Great Britain in 1988
by Ward Lock, an imprint of Cassell,
Villiers House, 41/47 Strand, London WC2N 5JE

Reprinted 1988, 1989, 1990 (twice)

Text filmset in Monophoto Sabon
by MS Filmsetting Limited, Frome, Somerset
Printed and bound in Great Britain
by William Collins Sons & Co Ltd, Glasgow

British Library Cataloguing in Publication Data

Lansbury, Angela
Wedding speeches and toasts
1. Public speaking   2. Weddings
I. Title
808.85'933   PN4121

ISBN 0-7063-6642-5

CONTENTS

INTRODUCTION

'You'll have to make a speech!' are words you may wish
never to hear. But whether you are the bride, bridegroom, bride's father, mother, best man, chief bridesmaid, matron of honour, or family friend, the occasion is
almost upon you and you may need to make a speech.
Have no fear. It can be fun, and this book is here to help
you.

Why make a wedding speech? To express thanks, give
information, and, quite simply, because it is a tradition.
And you also have a unique opportunity to pay public
compliments to those you love most.

What is a speech and what is a toast? You can have a
speech without a toast, and a toast without a speech, but
at a wedding it is usual to combine the two.

Traditionally, the first speech, usually given by the
bride's father or an old family friend ends with the
proposal of a toast to the health of the bride and
bridegroom. The second speech is given as a reply to the
first by the bridegroom and is concluded with the
proposal of a toast to the bridesmaids. The best man
then replies on behalf of the bridesmaids, and will
conclude his speech by proposing a toast to the parents
of the bride and groom.

The modern wedding, however, is much more flexible
and women are welcomed to play a part. The bride may
feel more comfortable making the speech on behalf of
herself and her new husband, for example. Or the job of
replying to the toast of the bridesmaids could be taken
on by chief bridesmaid rather than the best man. The
important thing to remember is to decide well in advance
who will be speaking when, and of course to let them
know so that they have plenty of time to prepare.

As well as giving general advice on the preparation

and delivery of a speech, this book includes sample speeches. These can be used to model your own speech on. In chapter 4 pre-wedding speeches, in particular those to be given at engagement parties and stag parties, are dealt with. In chapter 5 model speeches for the wedding day itself are given. Those in a hurry who want a readymade speech can start reading there. Afterwards, or instead, read through the chapters on the etiquette of who could and should speak, on preparing and delivering the speech, and the chapters on anecdotes and quotations in order to make your speech truly personal and original. Finally there is advice about ad libbing on the day, which can give you the confidence to cope with any unforeseen forthcoming disasters and delights.

ETIQUETTE

The purpose of etiquette is to provide an easy set of rules which we can follow when we are in a hurry and want to make sure that we do not give offence to anybody. For example, we would not wish to neglect to thank the hosts, or fail to recognize the presence and importance of an honoured guest. The rules are most useful on formal occasions like weddings, and particularly when they happen only once in a lifetime. But because lifestyles are changing constantly the rules of etiquette are changing too – a little slower than lifestyles perhaps, but still changing.

Social occasions are now more flexible, so that the bride or bride's mother can speak if she so wishes, and sometimes the best man can be a best girl! The bride may also be given away by her mother.

THE TIMING OF SPEECHES

Circumstances and ideas vary in different countries and the rules of speechmaking differ for different religions. When speeches are made after seated dinners at lengthy, formal wedding receptions, they begin after all eating at the formal meal has finished, and are preceded by the announcement from the toastmaster, 'Ladies and Gentlemen, you may now smoke.' If the meal finishes with tea or coffee and wedding cake, speeches will be made after the cutting of the cake. There is a natural tendency to call for speeches after the bride and groom have stood behind the cake to be photographed. It is easier to hold the attention of the diners at the end of the meal while they are seated, and still too full to want to get up and start dancing.

However, if the celebration is to continue all evening and the tea and coffee and wedding cake are to be served later, it is possible to delay the cutting of the cake until after the speeches which conclude the meal. Whatever the wedding organizers decide, it is important to let the toastmaster and the speechmakers know, so that they are prepared and do not disappear at the vital moment.

Let us suppose you have late guests arriving after the wedding meal. What do you do? At seated dinners the number of guests invited to the meal may be limited by the cost or the size of the hall. Sometimes the seated guests are just the closest family and friends, while other friends, children, neighbours and colleagues from work are invited for the dancing and party later in the day. A few guests who are invited to a midweek ceremony may not be able to leave work early, are delayed by rush hour traffic, or have to return home to change their clothes, and therefore they reach the reception after it has started.

Guests should not enter during speeches, distracting the audience and disconcerting the speakers. But it is also necessary to avoid keeping them standing outside in the rain, or waiting in draughty corridors feeling unwanted while the meal finishes or the speeches are in progress. The hotel or hall staff can arrange chairs, drinks, and someone to direct and greet the late arrivals, who can then view the wedding presents, or be introduced to each other until a suitable moment arrives for them to enter the dining hall. They should then not be left standing if other guests are seated, but shown to chairs on one side of the hall, or be directed to the seating plans so that they can fill the places kept for them, or go to seats left empty by 'no-shows' such as anyone taken ill at the last minute. You may wish to time the cake cutting and speeches so that later arrivals can enjoy them. The printed invitation can make any such timing clear.

What to Do at Buffets and Informal Weddings

At a buffet you ensure that elderly and infirm guests, and

those who have travelled long distances, have seats near the buffet table so that they are not obliged to stand for a long period. If there is no toastmaster, the best man, or woman, calls the attention of the guests to the start of the cake-cutting ceremony. The bride and groom pose for photographs to be taken by the official photographer and relatives who have brought their cameras. The chief bridesmaid, if she is not making a speech, can then lead the call for a speech.

THE TOASTMASTER

The first question you need to ask yourself is do you need a toastmaster? At a large wedding it is useful to have a toastmaster to announce guests on the receiving line. He will know the traditional way to announce titles, that Mr and Mrs John Smith are husband and wife, Mrs John Smith is without her husband John who is away on business, Mrs Anne Smith is a widow, or that Mr John Smith and Mrs Anne Smith are the elderly aunt and uncle, brother and sister, not married to each other. The toastmaster opens the proceedings and keeps them flowing smoothly. In his absence the task would fall to the best man.

There are other benefits from employing a toast-master. Since one essential quality of a good toastmaster is a loud voice, (which often goes with an imposing, extrovert personality) they will get attention faster than you can (an alternative way to get the attention of the audience is to ask the band, if you have one, to do a drum roll for you). However, to ensure that proceedings go as you would wish, give the toastmaster instructions in advance, rather than piecemeal later.

If a toastmaster attends, he will begin his duties by announcing the names of guests stepping forward to shake hands with the bridal party on the receiving line. Afterwards he will raise his voice and holler loud enough to be heard by the whole roomful of guests milling around chatting, perhaps talking excitedly with drinks in their hands, 'LADIES and GENTLEMEN! Pray be seated. DINNER is now being served!' When everyone has found their places he stands by the microphone at the top table, hammers on the table with a gavel, and announces loudly, 'Ladies and Gentlemen, Pray SILENCE for the Reverend John Smith, who will now say grace.'

If there is no toastmaster, the best man may introduce the minister more simply, 'Ladies and Gentlemen, Reverend John Smith will now say grace.' The best man should check in advance the correct title and form of address for the minister, Archbishop, Chief Rabbi, or whoever will be attending. Is it Reverend, the Reverend, Mr, Mrs, or what?

THE WHO AND WHEN OF SPEECHMAKING

The traditional order of toasts has a certain logic. The first speech leads up to a toast to bride and groom, the most important people of the day. In effect at a traditional first wedding they are the honoured guests of the hosts, her parents. But while as host her father can make a speech or toast to his new son-in-law, it would be a bit immodest for him to sing the praises of his own daughter, so often a friend of the family is chosen to make a speech and toast to both bride and groom, particularly if the father is going to speak later. The honour of making the first speech may go to the best speaker or the best friend, providing your choice keeps as many people as possible happy!

It falls to the groom to reply to the first speech on behalf of himself and his bride. Whom should he thank? Both his in-laws, especially if they've paid for or organized the wedding, and especially his mother-in-law. Who else has helped? Presumably the bridesmaids. So he ends with a toast to the bridesmaids and/or Matron of Honour.

The bride, however, may speak instead of her husband or as well as him. If there are no bridesmaids the groom can make a toast to his bride, who can speak next in reply. The bride can propose a toast to the bridegroom if the first toast was to her alone, or to the bridesmaids or Matron of Honour. Alternatively she can propose a toast to the family of the bridegroom, or if they are not present, to the guests.

The best man replies on behalf of the helpers (the bridesmaids). If there are no bridesmaids he does not have to speak, though he may wish to do so. The best man or the groom can end his speech with a toast to the hosts, and the bride's father or mother, or both, can reply.

An optional final toast to HM the Queen is made at most Jewish weddings in the UK. Lastly the best man or the toastmaster reads the telegrams in full if there are only a few, or reads the wittiest in full and then just gives the names of the senders of the others if there are many.

Variations to these customs can be made when there are no bridesmaids, or parents, or for a second marriage where the couple are paying for their own wedding.

When you have decided who is speaking, tell them all how many speakers there are and in which order they are speaking. Also check whom they will be toasting.

Surprise Announcements

The surprise delivery of a large gift, or the surprise arrival of a friend or relative from overseas, can be great fun. However, the best man or chief bridesmaid will have to take responsibility for the announcement, and the safekeeping of any gift. Most gifts are sent to the bride's mother's home in advance. That way the donor's cards are not muddled in the confusion of the day, and presents are kept safely and not left in hotels or halls where they might go astray.

It is the bride's day, and surprise announcements of

the engagements and forthcoming weddings of other guests might cause illwill. They could deflect attention from the bride. The announcement of the bride's sister's engagement would be acceptable, but only if the bride herself knows in advance and gladly agrees to the public announcement being made at her wedding.

Language Barriers
It can be a problem if, for example, the groom speaks no English: either he, or the bride and her family, may feel he ought to have the opportunity to speak at his own wedding, or that he has a duty to honour his hosts by thanking them publicly.

There are two solutions. Either he speaks in his own language and an interpreter delivers a translation; the translator can be the bride or another person. Or he can remain silent except for nodding, smiling and lifting his glass, allowing the bride to speak on their behalf, making due reference to him – my husband has asked me, etc.

The same system will be adopted if you have two receptions, one in each country. The speakers just have to do everything twice, taking note of which family is playing host.

INFORMAL RECEPTIONS

If your wedding guests are not seated in a reception hall but milling around a hotel or house your problem is to ensure that everyone is gathered in the right place at the right time to hear the speeches. You may have to tell guests in advance, 'We're cutting the cake and having the speeches in the dining room at half past,' then send the chief bridesmaid into the gardens if it is a fine day, and the other bridesmaids around the house, to inform stragglers that the speeches are about to be made.

Don't start the proceedings until you are sure that the speakers themselves are present as well as the hosts or anyone else who will be thanked or mentioned in the speeches. Keep the speeches short because one third of the audience can't see, one third can't hear, and one third are trying to locate a seat so that they will not drop their handbag, glass, or plate, when they clap you.

Even if you decide to dispense with speeches altogether, you may find that after the cake is cut the crowd of well-wishers start chanting, 'Speech! Speech!', so that at least the groom has to give a speech. Somebody will then decide to give an impromptu reply if the best man doesn't, which makes him feel he should have spoken. So if you are the best man, you might as well prepare a few words. You might then find that having gone to the trouble of preparing a good speech and a joke just in case, you decide that you might as well give the speech anyway!

AFTER THE PARTY

Souvenirs of the wedding may include photographs of the speakers delivering speeches, the guests standing around the happy couple with glasses raised, typed copies of the speech to go in the wedding album, or video recordings of the occasion.

When the party is over members of the bridal party, and guests, may want to go up to the speakers and personally thank them, complimenting them on a good, amusing speech. In addition the bride and groom or hosts could express thanks in the form of a short note and accompanying photo or small gift.

Following the honeymoon, a party is often held to show the family photos of the trip. At the same time if a video has been taken of the wedding the speakers will want to see themselves. Should they have made any small mistakes they will laugh and learn to improve next time, and if their performance was perfect they will be absolutely delighted.

PREPARING THE SPEECH

When first sitting down to write your speech it may be a good idea to ask yourself why you have been asked to speak? Is it because you are expected to express good wishes or thanks, or because you are old and wise and expected to give advice, or because you are an extrovert and known for being humorous, because you are closely related to the other members of the family, or because you are a friend who has known the bride and groom for many years? The answer to this question may suggest to you what sort of speech to give.

PLANNING YOUR SPEECH

It is important to leave yourself enough time before the wedding in order to give much consideration as to what you would like to say, to do any research necessary, as well as to write your speech and to perform any last minute pruning. Remember, a few scribbled notes will not suffice.

Length of Speech

It is important to decide the length of your speech before beginning to research and write it. Too short and it may seem rude, too long and it may bore the guests and dampen the proceedings. If you really *can't* decide, settle on about five minutes. As a rule of thumb, if the occasion is a very formal one it will demand a longer speech; an informal occasion is more flexible. Remember, your speech will reflect not only on those you are speaking about but upon yourself.

Gathering Information

Before even attempting to write your speech, take stock of the information you have to hand and see where the gaps occur. Only then should you set about researching in order to fill your speech out, make it interesting, witty, or whatever style of speech you would like to make. Beware, however, of drowning yourself in pages of notes. Panic will not be too far away if having collected all your information you have only a little time to write the speech.

Begin your research by looking for ideas on which you can expound and expand. For instance, the theme of marriage itself is always popular. You could research ideas on the history of marriage and interesting marriage customs both here and abroad.

In addition you could ask the parents of the bride and groom about their marriages. Did the marriage take place in wartime? Wearing similar clothes? With hundreds of guests? Enquire about the cake, photographer, transport, food, music, dancing, honeymoon destination, and first home. The living grandparents, uncles and aunts, may also have interesting stories about their weddings and marriages of friends, brothers, sisters and other relatives which took place in unusual or typically different circumstances in earlier days.

The best time to get people to talk about themselves is when you are sitting around the table over a meal or having tea, and when they are relaxed and are not likely to be diverted by other activities. Remember here that some people do not like seeing you write down their words for it interrupts their flow of thought. If you have a poor memory you could slip away for a moment and write yourself a quick note. Alternatively use a small tape recorder so that you can join in the conversation without notetaking. Reactions to tape recording differ. While a few people do not like tape recorders, others love to have what they said played back at a family party, and then argue and correct each other and make interesting extra comments.

From the family history you can learn about the

family's ancestors, where they have lived and worked, where they met, their education, work skills, achievements, hobbies, and character. Personal anecdotes can be added. You will need to strike a balance between personal and general remarks. It would be unfortunate if you generalized a great deal and delivered a speech which could have been given at anybody's wedding, when the bride and groom have fascinating family histories.

So make sure you persist even if your first enquiry produces no immediate result. You may find that the bride says, 'Don't bother to say anything about where I went to school and where we met. It's not really interesting.' If one of your subjects doesn't provide you with information, ask another. You might discover that someone else such as the bride's mother has really interesting revelations about the bride. Maybe despite or because of failing 'O' levels she went on to become the first woman engineer at her college because her earlier setbacks had made her determined to prove that she could succeed.

Make enquiries from both sides of the family. The discovery of the meaning of the family name may be news to the other side. And the countries all the grandparents came from could be quite interesting. But so is the fact that one or both families have lived in the same area for four generations. This is not the sort of news which would make the front pages of newspapers, but you can assume that on the day everyone will be interested in the bride and groom and their respective families.

The profession of the bride or groom may provide speech matter. If your subject has academic qualifications you could ask such questions as, 'How long did it take you to get your degree?'; 'What subject is your PhD in?'; 'How long have you been a member of the Architect's Association?'; 'Where did you study for the bar?'; 'How does the FBOA differ from the FSMC?'.

If the bride or groom or their families or ancestors are famous, it might be worth your while looking them up in Who's Who, and similar reference works, of which there are many editions covering authors, scientists, theatrical personages, and royalty.

COMPOSING AND PRUNING YOUR SPEECH

Work Out the Structure

Prune your notes if necessary and arrange them in the order in which you would like to use them. List the essentials to be included such as thanks and the toast. Only then should you consider your opening remarks.

Avoid stereotyped ideas if possible. Have you talked only about the bride cooking for the bridegroom when you know she is a career girl and a women's libber, and if *she* is not some of the audience will be?

Delete anything in dubious taste. If in doubt, leave it out. Avoid negatives, regrets, criticisms of others, making the families appear foolish, making yourself appear foolish, and anything vague.

Remove rude jokes and deliberate sexual innuendos, and also watch out for unintended double entendres which might make inebriated members of the audience laugh when you are being serious and sincere. You can cause hysterics all round with such apparently innocent remarks as the bride's father saying, 'I didn't expect to enjoy myself so much. You don't enjoy things so much when you get older.' (I should know. I was the bride.)

Reading Your Speech Aloud

Read the speech aloud to yourself first to be sure the sentences are not too long and you are not stumbling over them. It must sound like something you would say spontaneously. Later when you are satisfied, you might read it to a limited number of people – just one or two.

You don't want all the wedding party to have heard the speech in advance of the wedding.

Improving the Style

Change words or phrases you have repeated. Enliven cliches by subtly altering them if possible. Explain jargon and foreign phrases.

Change repetitions by looking for new words with the same meaning in Roget's *Thesaurus*. Paperback copies are available from bookshops. A dictionary of synonyms and antonyms might also be useful. And if you intend to compose your own poems, limericks or verses, a songwriter's rhyming dictionary would be invaluable.

For an ordinary wedding a colloquial way of speaking will be suitable. However, should you be called upon to speak at a grand, formal wedding you may feel that a more erudite speech is required. Forms of address and titles for important personages can be found in reference books.

To eliminate or locate colloquial words there are dictionaries of slang. For the transatlantic marriages, several dictionaries of American expressions are available, enabling you to eliminate Americanisms, explain yourself to American listeners, or make jokes about the differences between Americanisms and conventional English language.

Anticipating Little Problems

Try to anticipate any controversial subjects and disasters you might have to mention, or avoid mentioning, in the course of your speech.

Make yourself a troubleshooter's checklist. What would I say if: her Dad died; his parents couldn't attend; her parents didn't attend; the best man didn't arrive because his plane from India was delayed; it turned out to be the groom's second wedding, although it is her first; the Matron of Honour didn't turn up because she was ill; the groom dried up and forgot to compliment the bridesmaids so I couldn't thank him?

You may also have to state facts which are obvious to you, but not to cousins who have not seen the family for several years. You might also have to avoid stating the obvious.

Final Check

Finally, check that your speech fits in with the speeches and toasts given by others. Be sure that you know the name of the previous speaker so that you can say, 'Thank you, George,' confident that his name is not James. And if your friend, the bridegroom, or the bride's father-in-law or another older man is usually called 'Al', on this occasion should you be calling him by his full name, (and if so, is that short for Albert, Alfred, Ali, Alexis, Alexander, or, even more formally, Mr Smith?

DELIVERING THE SPEECH

Perhaps the most important rule to follow when delivering your speech is to make sure that you are relaxed right from the start. With this in mind take a few relaxing deep breaths before you stand to speak and then make sure you are standing comfortably. Above all, if you are well prepared you will be more relaxed.

IMPORTANT TECHNIQUES

Being Heard

Being audible depends on your ability to project your voice and correctly using a microphone if one is available. To begin, take a deep breath before you start so that you don't run out of breath in the middle of the sentence. Do not lose interest and let the end of a sentence fade away as you scan your notes for the next remark. Throughout the speech you must speak loudly, aiming to be heard by the person at the far end of the room.

Keep your head up. Don't talk to your tie or your toes. Don't mumble. If you have an audience of about a hundred people at least one will have hearing problems, difficulty understanding English, or difficulty understanding your accent. That is another reason for keeping your head up, so that such people can see your lips moving as well as hearing what you are saying. If they have to turn to their neighbour and ask for a repetition of what you just said, the resulting muttering will also prevent other members of the audience from hearing what you say next. If you know in advance that some people are hard of hearing you can seat them accordingly.

You must get the attention of your audience right at

the start of the speech – then hold the audience's attention during the speech. Their attention will wander if you pause to look at your notes, and again the muttering of some will prevent others from hearing. However, you should pause after jokes for two reasons. Firstly, so that those who are slow know when the joke ends, or can have a moment to reflect and catch the subtleties of any double entendre. Secondly, if the joke is so successful that it gets a lot of laughter you do not want to rush on so fast that your next words cannot be heard.

Using a Microphone

When you arrive at the reception check whether a microphone will be available. But be prepared and able to speak without it just in case it is not available or an electrical fault develops.

At a seated dinner the speakers are usually at the top table and the microphone is nearby and can be handed to each speaker. But if the first speaker is not seated at the top table there may be a pause while he walks to the microphone. If a delay occurs between one speaker and the next the audience may start talking so that the next speaker will have to recapture their attention. A toast-master has his own techniques. He may bang on the table with a mallet and then shout, 'Pray silence for THE BRIDEGROOM!'

The first speaker should not be the one who discovers whether the microphone is working at all. Perhaps the best man could take on the responsibility of arriving before the guests and checking the microphone. However, the best man is sometimes asked to stay behind at the church, organizing transport and ensuring that the last guest does not get stranded when all the cars have departed. In this case another usher or bridesmaid could take over the duty of checking the microphone.

The usual technique for checking that the microphone is set to the correct level after the audience arrives is to call, 'Can you all hear me?' Since those at the front shout loudly, you won't necessarily know that those at the back can't. A more interesting variation would be, 'Hello. I'm going to check that the microphone works before I start. Could those on the back table shout, "Hello".' Another variation would be, 'Hello, I just want to check you all got here all right. Did the relatives from Manchester arrive?' (Check the table plan in advance to see who is on the back table or tables.) 'Yes? Good. Now I can start.'

Microphones can make high pitched screaming noises called 'howl', and they are due to feedback. The cure is to move the microphone or to move the loudspeakers, which is not always practical, or adjust the microphone volume to a lower level. The adjusting device is located on the amplifier that the microphone is plugged into. If you cannot correct it, anyone experienced in public speaking, such as the toastmaster, should be able to remedy the problem. Sophisticated systems do not present this problem at all.

When you are testing the microphone, start softly and then speak louder. You don't want to start by bellowing so loudly that people shrink in alarm. If you see the audience cowering back, you are too loud. Alternatively, see if they are straining to hear you. Some experienced speakers ask a friend to stand against the back wall and signal with hands facing forward by their ears if you need to speak louder, and with hands horizontal if you should speak more softly.

Ensure that you are not so near the microphone that it picks up every sound including heavy breathing and muttered asides. Neither stand so far away that it cannot pick up your voice. The other thing to avoid is swaying backward and forward so that you are alternately bellowing and whispering, fading out or disappearing entirely at intervals like a badly tuned radio station!

Don't be frightened by hearing the sound of your own

voice magnified. Everybody wants to hear you because they are your friends, or because they are friends of the happy couple and want to hear what you have to say about them. If you practise listening to yourself speaking on tape, you will be used to the timbre or magnification of your voice.

Emphasis and Speed

The pace of your delivery is important. Don't gallop through your speech as if you can't wait to finish it and get away. Vary the pace and speed; if the sentences are varied in length this helps. If you are inclined to race along like a commentator at a horse race try to slow down and introduce a pause or two. But if you have a slow, sad delivery, try to talk faster, and reach a climax at the end of one or two sentences, at least as you reach the end of the speech.

Introduce some changes in emotion: gratitude, surprise, amusement, and seriousness. This will be partly dictated by the text. But if you have practised on a tape recorder and you discover that you are talking in a monotonous, even tone, try reading the speech putting emphasis on certain words. Decide which is the most important word in the sentence. Should the sentence, 'I have never seen such a beautiful bride' be read as, 'I have NEVER seen such a beautiful bride', or 'I have never seen such a BEAUTIFUL bride'? Or even '"I" have never seen such a beautiful bride'. You could even underline key phrases or words in your speech notes. Your facial expressions can help to emphasize parts of your speech too: try smiling, scowling, or raising your eyebrows.

You will find that ease of emphasis comes more readily if you are not standing stiffly to attention while delivering your speech. A rehearsal ploy used by actors may be useful here. Stand and rehearse in front of a full length mirror, checking that you are smiling and making the right gestures, including lifting your glass sufficiently high and forward when proposing the toast so that you convey enthusiasm.

Confidence

If you are lacking in confidence ask yourself what most frightens you. If it is finding a good speech to interest and amuse the audience, then with preparation you should have solved that problem already. Is it having people looking at you or having to speak to a large crowd when you have never done that before? Perhaps you think that some of the more important people present will think your speech is not good enough. If you are afraid of talking to a crowd, remember that this is not a crowd of strangers, but a crowd of friends. Your audience is not critical. They want you to succeed. They are out to have a good time. They are expecting you to say something nice. You can rely on their goodwill.

Where you look when making your speech can be a help. Start by concentrating on one person, perhaps addressing your mother or your best friend and then, when you see them smiling back and you gather confidence, turn to the rest of the audience. In fact, to get confidence when rehearsing your speech, read it to the person who is most likely to be encouraging.

Again it will be your posture that will help you and give an impression of confidence, or lack of it, to your audience. Walk tall if you have to walk towards the microphone. Don't sink into your shoulders as if one of the chandeliers is about to descend and hit you on the head. Stretch up as if you are trying to reach something on the top shelf of the kitchen at home and you know you are going to succeed.

Try not to look anxious and afraid. Smile. If you smile, other people will smile back. Look at people as you pass them and you will see that they are smiling at you. This is a happy occasion and a party occasion so almost certainly they will be smiling!

Conquering Nerves

There are many techniques you can use beforehand to help you relax. It could be having a good night's sleep the night before, playing tennis or taking a sauna, losing weight or having a stiff drink just before you begin. For those who know how, doing yoga for half an hour in the morning, or meditating in a darkened room for ten minutes just before giving the speech will assist, or perhaps it will require nothing more than taking a deep breath before you speak.

PRACTISING PUBLIC SPEAKING

If you have never stood up in front of other people and given a speech, you could take a course in public speaking, or buy a book on the subject and go through the techniques they practise. This may seem rather excessive just for giving one speech, but if this is your first and you speak well, you may well be asked to give speeches later at other weddings and functions. And if you enjoy it you may even volunteer to do so. A public speaking course may be very useful for your career, and will give you confidence in general, but if you have no spare cash or time for a course because the wedding is approaching, you might try practising public speaking by yourself.

Since general public speaking courses are not preparing you to give a particular speech, but to give speeches in general, the first task is simply to get you to stand up in a room full of people and ask you to speak about anything you like for three minutes. You could try this with several subjects. Pick three subjects you know well, such as your hobby, your job, and your mother. For example, 'Ladies and Gentlemen, I am very glad to have this opportunity of telling you about my magnificent stamp collection. I have been collecting stamps of the world since I was eight-years old and specialize in, etc.' Or, 'Ladies and Gentlemen, I am delighted to be invited to tell you about the amusing experiences I have had while travelling/teaching as a, etc.' Perhaps, 'Ladies and Gentlemen, everybody thinks their own mother is something special and I am no exception. My mother . . .' You can either record this and play it back or stand in front of a friend and let them criticize and make helpful suggestions.

Rehearsing in the Reception Hall
Most people are slightly nervous in unfamiliar situations ranging from opening the door into a strange room to having a job interview. If being in unfamiliar places worries you, you might find it helpful to visit the reception hall in advance and even to stand where you will be standing to give the speech and rehearse the opening sentence.

PRE-WEDDING SPEECHES

Various kinds of engagement and pre-wedding parties can be held. An engagement party can be arranged to introduce families and friends to the other families, and inform everyone that the young couple are now attached. If the engagement period is to be protracted because the couple are young or studying, there may be a big party not unlike a small-scale version of the wedding at which the future bride has a chance to display her ring to well-wishers and acquire presents for the new home, for which the guests must be thanked.

More than one bride's father has been heard to say that he did not want to have a large engagement party if the wedding was to follow within a year because that would involve him in the organization and expense of 'two weddings'. That is why the bridegroom's family hosts the engagement party.

An engagement party is traditionally held by the future bridegroom's parents, but there is no reason why one should not be held by the bride's family, or by both families in their own home or elsewhere, particularly if the two families live in different areas.

Unlike wedding reception speeches the engagement party speeches are usually very short, merely introducing the young couple, expressing pleasure at the engagement, and wishing them happiness. A parent of the bride or groom speaks or, if there are no parents present, another older relative playing host can make the speech.

ENGAGEMENT PARTY SPEECHES

To the happy couple by the groom's father/mother (or the bride's)

I am delighted to welcome you to meet Steven's fiancée Annabelle and her family (or Annabelle's fiancé Steven and his family). They hope to marry next June, or sooner if they find a house. It is lovely to see you all, and so many friends from their old school and college and Steven's office (or from Annabelle's old school). Thank you so much for your good wishes. I hope everybody's got a glass of champagne – Have you? Good! Because I would like you to join me in wishing every happiness to Annabelle and Steven.

To Annabelle and Steven.

Reply and thanks to the host and guests by bride/groom and toast to the other family

I want to thank Mum and Dad for throwing this lovely party so that you could meet Annabelle and her family (or Steven and his family). Thank you all for coming this evening, and for bringing such generous presents. I'd like you to drink a toast to Annabelle's parents Betty and Jim (or Steven's parents John and Clare).

To Betty and Jim (or John and Clare).

Thanks and toast to hosts by the other family

I'd like to thank Betty and Jim for organizing this wonderful party to give both of our families the ideal opportunity to get to know each other. And thank you everyone for the lovely presents for our new home. Please join me in wishing good health to Betty and Jim.

To Betty and Jim.

BACHELOR PARTIES

Stag parties and hen parties used to be held the night before the wedding, the last opportunity for the girls and boys to go out, or stay at home, with friends of their own sex. The timing of these parties, and their occasionally unfortunate results have made it very unpopular to hold them immediately before the wedding.

An innocuous bachelor party can be held either at a respectable restaurant where food is served along with drink, or with food and family present at home. The entertainment is the pleasure of reminiscing with one's friends and making a couple of witty speeches. If this is thought too tame, a lively and amusing party can be held at home or in a room at a sports club along the lines of a fancy dress party, again with humorous speeches.

The responsibility of the brother, sister, or best friend who organizes the bachelor party is to ensure that it is a happy event for the guest of honour, and that the jokes, entertainment and gifts do not embarrass those present or absent who will hear about the party later, or imperil the relationship between the engaged couple. To organize the event successfully, make an amusing speech, and get the right balance between outrageous fun and good taste, will indicate to the bride or groom that you can be relied upon to perform well as best man or bridesmaid at the subsequent wedding.

BACHELOR PARTY SPEECHES

Speech by best friend to bridegroom-to-be

We are here to say goodbye to our brother, Steven, who is departing for the land of the married. We all knew that Steven was regarded as an eligible bachelor, but we didn't think that marriage was what he was eligible for. We tried to dissuade Steven from marrying, but alas to no avail. We warned him that a husband is a glorified handyman, that he will be spending his weekends painting, decorating, gardening, and maintaining the car. He will be abandoning happy Saturday afternoons spent watching football, and instead spend them shopping, spending money. If he cannot afford a dishwasher he will be a dishwasher. Sundays will no longer be a day of rest spent playing cricket or sailing, but devoted to visiting in-laws. Evenings at the pub or the bar will have to be abandoned and he will stay at home, opening bottles for others to drink. To all this, he said, and I quote, 'Rubbish.' So you see, his vocabulary has changed already! He continued, 'You are not married. How do you know?'

So we sought wiser men than ourselves who have trodden the same path he proposes to take. W. C. Fields said that women are like elephants, very nice to look at, but he wouldn't want to own one. A look at our former friends who have married will show that marriages are made in heaven, to make life hell below.

Alternatively choose a quotation from the selection in the chapter entitled Quotations.

Many young ladies will mourn Steven's departure. He was all things to all young women. Sometimes they were queuing to telephone him. In fact a lady who looked like Mae West was hiding in the phone box at the car park waiting to see him as we came along tonight. She is still waiting, alas in vain.

We, too, have failed. He remains unconvinced. To him an evening with one woman is worth an evening with ten of us. She must be a truly wonderful girl. We shall never know. So we have gathered here this evening to spend a last evening telling jokes with our friend, who is unfettered by responsibilities. We decided to present him with a small token which he can take to his new life, and keep in memory of his bachelor days and the friends he has left behind. Unfortunately when we went into the shop to buy his gift we met a couple of his ex-girlfriends who insisted on coming along to remind him of the girls he is leaving behind, and to present him with a small, but wonderfully-packaged gift, a token of our friendship. Steven – Here they are!

Two male friends dressed in drag appear, possibly as twin brides, preferably in long dresses or other outfits that keep them well covered to prevent any incidents among their own group or from outsiders. They present the gift. It should be something useful for setting up home, if only a rather expensive bottle-opener, possibly with other small mementoes of his favourite bachelor activities or sport such as golf balls, presented inside something amusing and clearly feminine but not in bad taste, such as a pair of stockings, with a blue garter for him to give to his bride for the wedding so that she can wear 'something borrowed, something blue'.

An alternative would be a huge gift, something large which the drag brides have difficulty getting through the door, such as a golfing umbrella, or a garden umbrella if the couple hope to move from bachelor flats into a house. It could be extended to look even longer, and presented with the words that we wanted to give you 'a small gift' or a gift 'big enough for two'. I am sure that the jokes which this will inspire can be left to the inspiration of the moment.

Speech of reply by the bachelor boy

Dear Friends. I appreciate your concern for me. I, too, am concerned for you. Your gifts are very welcome and will be appreciated by Annabelle as well as myself. Boys/Guys/Mates, you don't know what you are missing. While I am tucked up by my warm fire being waited on hand and foot, you will be out in your cars touring the streets with nowhere to go, wishing in vain for a lovely girl to console you and end your loneliness.

How can a football or a golfball be compared to a girl? Those of you who still do not know the difference, I hope will one day find out the good news, and meet the girl of their dreams. In only five weeks I shall be getting married to Annabelle. We look forward to seeing you all at our wedding, and later to welcoming you to dinner in our new home. Who knows, at the wedding or at our place you may meet the girl who may change your mind about the joys of remaining a bachelor. Annabelle and I have 'got a little list' of eligible bachelors, and you are all on it. We bachelors have had many good times together, and we shall have more. They are not over. I am not halving my friends, but doubling them. Please raise your glass and drink a toast to Alan who has organized this party for me. May he enjoy happy bachelor days, but not too many, before he realizes the error of his ways and is claimed by one of the angels on Earth. To Alan. (An alternative toast could be to friendships which endure forever.)

Speech by best friend to bride-to-be

We tried to dissuade Annabelle from marrying, but alas to no avail. We warned her that a wife's work is never done. She is chained to the kitchen sink and washing socks. Unpaid secretary, social organizer, babysitter, cook, etcetera. When we told her this she said, and I quote, 'Phooey!'

There are many young men who will mourn her departure from the ranks of the available, ah (sigh), some of whom had fond memories of her, others, merely hopes. She was a very popular girl. Men flocked into her office. We realized why when we called. She had taken the sign MEN from the Gents, and put it on her office door.

But now that Steven has claimed her, those days are gone. Her parents and flatmates look forward to the recovery of their telephones and bathrooms.

We must admit that it looks to us like a very good match, and it is only because she is marrying Steven that she has such an idealized view of what men and marriage are really like. Does she not know the truth, that after marriage, life changes. Men can be late. Women cannot. We are duty bound to warn her of what others who married have said. But since we have failed to persuade her to stay single, we can only wish her well, and give her this small token of our good wishes for her future, in memory of our happy bachelor days together.

The girls bringing in the parcel could dress up like the bridegroom-to-be, taking his work or hobby as the theme, or like any male characters such as footballers, policemen or policewomen wearing sunglasses, gorillas with cigars, city gents in bowler hats, or a spoof pop group of boys in short trousers and caps singing, 'Will you still need me when I'm sixty-four?'. The parcel presented should be amusing, either an unusual shape, or several boxes inside each other so that the gift takes a while to find. The gift presented should be one of value and usefulness for setting up home (so that she is not disappointed), perhaps with a memento of her bachelor days, such as a cassette by her favourite pop singers, but inside a container gift which is a joke, e.g. a silver cake slice, or selection of kitchen implements, or telephone address book, plus cassettes in the bottom of a pair of large man's football socks (the correct size to fit her husband to be), or a pair of pillowcases embroidered 'his' and 'hers'. There should be a card signed by all the friends.

Speech of reply by bachelor girl
Dear Friends. I appreciate your message of goodwill, and your charming gifts. Don't you dare tell Steven that you found this pair of red socks under my bed! I shall always remember you, the way you look tonight! We have had a lot of fun together and we still shall. You'll all be at my wedding in six weeks/six months time, and frequent guests at my house, and in my garden. I shall throw my bouquet to one of you at the wedding and who knows, there might be another wedding in the not too distant future for somebody. My mother says, there's one for

everyone. Let's all have a drink together, I hope all my girlfriends will meet steady boyfriends, but as Helen organized this party and is going to be my chief bridesmaid, I'd like to wish happiness to Helen. To Helen. (An alternative toast would be, 'To friendship. May good friends stay together forever'.)

WEDDING SPEECHES

The following samples speeches are to suit different situations and speakers. Choose the most appropriate speech and substitute your own details. Alternatively pick up a pen and a piece of paper and compose your own speech immediately after reading all these for inspiration.

TOAST TO THE BRIDE AND GROOM

(Brief toast at an informal wedding party.)

I would like to propose a toast to Annabelle and Steven, wishing them much joy and happiness for their future together. May all their troubles be little ones. To Annabelle and Steven.

TOAST TO THE BRIDE AND GROOM

(A brief, simple, direct speech for the bride's father.)

Reverend Brown, Ladies and Gentlemen, all my guests, I cannot tell you how pleased I am today to see my daughter Annabelle looking so radiantly happy, as she begins life as the wife of Steven. My wife and I do not feel that we are losing Annabelle, but entrusting her to Stephen's good care. During the last few months as we have got to know him better, he has shown himself to be exactly the sort of person we had hoped Annabelle would marry – charming, sincere, reliable – with a clear idea of what he wants from life and how to achieve it. I know that his many friends and family, as well as those who have only recently met him, think that this must be one of those marriages that are made in heaven, and will want to join me in wishing Steven and Annabelle a long and happy married life together. So please stand and raise your glasses, and drink to the health and happiness of Annabelle and Steven. (Pause.)

To Annabelle and Steven.

TOAST TO THE BRIDE AND GROOM

(Longer, personalized speech by old friend or relative when bride's father is present but does not make a speech.)

Annabelle's father, George, and her mother, Martha, have done me the honour of offering me the opportunity to make a speech on this wonderful occasion and propose a toast to Annabelle and Steven. When I asked why they chose me, George said, because you are the President of the Oxford Drama Club/my bank manager/my oldest friend/the boss/have known us for twenty-five years/you are the tallest/you have the loudest voice/, and Martha said, because you have known Annabelle since she was fourteen/a baby/a child/all her life/at school/at college/you tell the best jokes. I have seen Annabelle acting in school plays/at the drama club on many occasions but today she doesn't need to act, she has a starring role.

Seriously, over the years I have seen Annabelle develop many talents and accomplishments. She has won prizes for (drama/music/essay-writing/cookery/coming top of her class in school, been awarded the first grade in music/drama, studied nursing/teaching/ballet/ice-skating/ French and management/interviewing/accounting, learned how to drive/ski/sail/swim/dance/surf/, followed her interests in travelling/bridge-playing/ opera/the orchestra/film and reading science fiction/ historical novels/biographies, as well as finding time to raise money for charity/do voluntary work with handicapped children/attend church functions regularly/ design clothes/paint/draw and to help in her family's shop/business/company/restaurant.

It was while she was at school/college/work, that she met Steven who was studying/working/travelling.

Though Steven had not yet qualified as a doctor/passed his A levels/opened his restaurant/learned to tell the difference between a gasket and a sprocket, it was obvious that they had much in common. (*Or:* At first it didn't look as if they had much in common.) But as they got to know each other Annabelle discovered that Steven liked the arts as much as the sciences/hiking as well as driving/driving cars as well as repairing them. And Steven learned that Annabelle could pilot a plane/ice a cake/run a playgroup/speak fluent French. And when Steven learned that Annabelle/Annabelle's father/mother/brother was an MP/barrister/had the best collection of Beatles records, that clinched it.

These young people have a bright future ahead of them, a wonderful career/job/home planned in London/New York/Sydney. And I am sure you will want to join me in wishing them every success and happiness in their new venture and marriage. Please raise your glasses and drink to the health and prosperity of Annabelle and Steven. (Pause.)

To Annabelle and Steven.

TOAST TO THE BRIDE AND GROOM

(Relative's/friend's speech when the bride's father is recently deceased.)

It is my great pleasure to be here with you on this happy occasion and to help Annabelle and Steven celebrate their marriage. I have known Annabelle and her parents for many years, since I/we/they came to live in London/Glasgow/Cardiff.

Annabelle's late father, George, used to enjoy a game of football/a game of golf/fixing the car on Saturday afternoons, and we spent many happy hours together sailing/relaxing often accompanied by Steven. I remember George saying that Steven seemed to be a very pleasant/good-natured/hard-working/ambitious/talented young man. I know George and Steven got on well and George would have been delighted to have seen this happy day. Although we miss George's presence, and his unfailing good humour, we know that he was looking forward to this wedding and we have fulfilled his hopes and wishes, and in a sense he is with us here today in our memories of him.

He would have been very satisfied to know what a comfort Steven has been to our family, how understanding, how supportive a friend in time of need, a valuable help to us in everything from fixing the car, taking over day to day decisions affecting the business/work/Annabelle's job, to just being there when we wanted advice and assistance. The wedding was postponed, but Annabelle is a girl well worth waiting for. Doesn't she look a picture today? George would have been proud of her, as I am sure Steven is. And it is with every confidence that I tell you I am sure that this young couple will have a very happy marriage, and I would ask you to join me in wishing them both a long, happy, and prosperous future together. Please stand and lift your glasses. I propose a toast – to Annabelle and Steven. (Lift glass in air and wait for everybody to stand and raise glasses.)

To Annabelle and Steven.

TOAST TO THE BRIDE AND GROOM

(Suitable for an older man addressing a large, distinguished audience.)

Ladies and Gentlemen, it is always a pleasure to attend a wedding. They say that the world loves a lover and I think this is true. Marriage is the expression of love, and also the start of a lifelong adventure. Plato said, 'The beginning is the most important part of the work'. If that is the case, then Annabelle and Steven have been fortunate in enjoying the most wonderful beginning. They already have most of the good gifts one would wish upon a young couple. Annabelle is a beautiful bride, Steven is a handsome husband, and both come from secure family homes where their parents have set examples of what a good marriage should be.

A good marriage is not something you can create on your own without help from your partner. It is a joint venture. Marriage is like a journey in a boat. You cannot drill a hole in the boat and when water floods in say to your companion, 'It's nothing to do with you, the water is coming in on my side of the boat.' You must row in the same direction. In fact love has been defined as not looking at each other, but looking in the same direction.

If marriage is a boat, then many of us are in the same boat! Annabelle and Steven, you are embarking on a wonderful journey, and you have many friends who will support you, and help you, and wish you well. I would now like to ask everyone in this room to stand with me, and raise their glasses. (Pause briefly until noise of moving chairs ceases.) I propose a toast to the long life, health, wealth, and happy marriage, of Annabelle and Steven.

To Annabelle and Steven!

TOAST TO THE BRIDE AND GROOM

(By the best man or best girl.)

It gives me special pleasure to be present at the wedding of my good friends Annabelle and Steven, because I introduced them at the Dashing Disco/Royal Hotel/Country Club and because I have known both of them for many years at school/the tennis club. May their lives continue with equal joy and may they share many happy occasions and reunions such as this with our families and friends. Here's to Annabelle and Steven.

BEST MAN'S TOAST TO BRIDE AND GROOM

('Impromptu' speech at a very small wedding without bridesmaids.)

This is a lovely small, intimate gathering of friends, which is just the way Annabelle and Steven wanted it to be. And we appreciate how honoured we are to be among the select few who they chose to share this very special occasion with them. Everyone here is a close friend or relative and we all have personal knowledge of Annabelle's unique qualities, her kindness, her gift for creating a happy atmosphere and her loyal friendship. And we are delighted that she is marrying Steven, who is so loved/admired by his family and close friends and is respected by all of us for his hard work/talents/skills/ zest for life. He shares many of her good qualities and they both deserve all the good things in life. So let's wish them both a very happy married life together. Has everyone got a drink? Good.

To Annabelle and Steven.

TOAST TO THE BRIDE'S PARENTS

(Groom's speech, replying to first toast to bride and groom, a longer, humorous speech.)

Reverend Brown, Ladies and Gentlemen, (Pause). Thank you very much, George, for those kind words. It goes almost without saying how pleased I am to be here today. In order not to dull your pleasure I intend to only speak for a few minutes in case we all get snowed in/melt away in the heat! We couldn't have wished for better weather – perfect sunshine, just the right start for a wedding day and honeymoon/the most beautiful, romantic white Christmas.

As you all know Annabelle has been a much sought after girl/woman, but I'm pleased to announce the winner of the competition, me. There are no runners up, or associated prizes.

My new mother-in-law, Martha, has worked long and hard for many months to prepare this wonderful occasion, all the little details such as these beautiful flower/cake decorations were planned by her, and my father-in-law has taken on his second mortgage without complaint, like the good-natured man he is. I am very pleased to be part of the same family and to know that my parents feel the same.

Speaking of whom, today represents a great occasion for both my parents, being the culmination of many years of planning of a different sort. They have prepared me well, supported me through university, taught me the difference between right and wrong, so that I know which I am enjoying at any given time!

Annabelle is beautiful, intelligent, and hard working. The list of her good qualities is extremely long. Unfortunately I cannot read her handwriting.

I would like to thank you all for your presence – in both senses of the word, but especially for the smiling faces I see in front of me. I am particularly pleased that Aunt Alice managed to make the long journey down to Surrey from Aberdeen for this occasion, and we are all delighted that Annabelle's sister, Sharon, flew all the way from Australia to join us and be such a charming bridesmaid. Of course she had a 'little help' – quite a big help, actually, from Tracey, who looked so sweet holding Annabelle's train.

My best man, Alan, has made everything go smoothly, and made his contribution to what has seemed the perfect day.

(Alternative ending: Finally, I must pay tribute to the bridesmaids Sharon, Natalie, Margaret and Sue whose invaluable support has helped to make this day so successful.)

If there are no bridesmaids, the toast is to his parents-in-law as follows:

In conclusion, thank, you, everybody, for listening, and I hope you are having a wonderful afternoon/evening and are all as happy as we are today. Would you kindly stand and raise your glasses and drink a toast to the health of your hosts, two wonderful people, George and Martha. (Pause.)

To George and Martha!

TOAST TO BRIDEGROOM AND BOTH FAMILIES

(Informal toast by the bride.)

I'd like to propose a toast to the most wonderful man in the world, my new husband, Steven. I'd also like to thank his parents for what they have contributed over the years to make him the person he is, supporting him through college, and also for making me such a welcome member of their family. I must also thank my parents for everything they have done for me and especially this wonderful event, my wedding to Steven. May we all meet on many more happy occasions.

To Steven.

TOAST TO THE BRIDESMAIDS

(Bridegroom's speech in reply to toast to the bride and groom, a brief but sincere speech.)

My wife and I (pause for laughter), thank you for your kind words. It is wonderful to be surrounded by so many friends and good wishes. We have been overwhelmed by the kindness and help we have received, the generous gifts, and the people who have made extra contributions on this, our special day. I must mention the bridesmaids who have done so much to help my wife, and added glamour to the photographs which will remind us of this very happy occasion.

To the bridesmaids!

TOAST TO GROOM'S FAMILY

(By the bride's father, replying to the groom's toast to the bride's parents who are hosts, giving personal family marriage details.)

Thank you, Steven. As you know Annabelle is our only daughter, so this will be our only chance to stage such a lovely wedding. And we did not want to miss the opportunity of having such a wonderful day, complete with the white wedding car. When my parents' generation were marrying back in the 1920s not everyone had cars and the best man's responsibility was to organize transport for all the guests. After the ceremony the bridal couple rushed to the photographer's studio to have their portrait taken, before joining their guests who were waiting for the wedding meal. For each generation the circumstances are different. Now we can have a photographer visiting us to make a video, so that we can remember this magical day for the rest of our lives.

Martha and I married during the Second World War, as did Steven's parents, when wedding couples needed clothing coupons from all their relatives to make the wedding dress and wedding suits, which had to be of sensible material so that they could be worn again. Everybody saved all their food coupons for the wedding cake. Since you could not go abroad you honeymooned on the south coast at resorts such as Bournemouth where there was barbed wire on the beaches. Despite that, Martha and I had a wonderful wedding, and were very grateful that when other families were separated, we had the opportunity to be together. But I think you will understand why we do not regret staging a grand wedding for Annabelle and Steven.

For us this has been a second chance, our only chance, to enjoy a wedding with all the luxuries and trimmings, and all our family around us. We want Annabelle and Steven to enjoy the things we never had, not to take them for granted, but to appreciate how lucky they are to be able to celebrate like this surrounded by their families and friends.

I know that Steven's parents understand how glad we are to do whatever we can for our daughter, and their son. We are very pleased to have Gregory and Gillian and their family here to celebrate with us. Their generous support and presence, joining in enthusiastically with everything we planned, has enabled us to truly enjoy this day. So please join me in drinking a toast to the health of my son-in-law's parents, Gregory and Gillian.

To Gregory and Gillian.

On a second or subsequent marriage it is frequently said that a wedding speech should make no reference to previous spouses, nor children of earlier marriages unless they are junior pages and need to be acknowledged and welcomed, or even the fact that either party has been married before. In theory you can use the usual wedding speeches, simply omitting any references to white weddings. However, rather than having the guests whispering conspiratorially amongst themselves the unmentionable secret that this is a second marriage, some speakers prefer a more direct and honest approach. This particularly applies where there is no question of a divorced previous spouse. It may be felt desirable to inform guests that one party was previously a devoted husband or wife, a widow or widower, who after years of loneliness should be congratulated on at last having found happiness again.

TOAST TO BRIDE AND GROOM (SECOND MARRIAGE)

(Short, happy, slightly humorous speech for a bride enjoying her first marriage to a divorced man.)

Annabelle, for you this is a first marriage and a time of

excitement and hope. For Steven it is a second marriage. He liked marriage so much that despite all the difficulties of his first attempt, when he met you he decided to try it again.

Annabelle, you may not realize it, but you are gaining the advantage of marrying a man who has had the sharp corners rubbed off him. A mature specimen. A vintage blend.

We hope that you will always enjoy life together, a very long and happy life together, and that you will always retain the enthusiasm of this new start, and remember the joy and delight of finding each other, which is so evident today. So we will all raise our glasses to you and toast your future.

To Annabelle and Steven.

TOAST TO BRIDE AND GROOM

(Short, happy, slightly humorous speech when the groom is marrying for the first time to a divorced woman.)

Steven, for you this is a first marriage and a time of expectation and hope. For Annabelle it is a second marriage. You must be especially proud today, because she liked you so much that despite all the difficulties of her first marriage, when she met you she decided to try it again. What an honour!.

Annabelle, you have the advantage of experience. Steven, you may not realize it, but you are gaining many advantages by marrying a mature woman. Vintage. We hope that both of you will always enjoy married life, a very long and happy life together. And that you will always retain the enthusiasm of this new start, and remember the joy and delight of finding each other, which is so evident today. So we will all raise our glasses to you and toast your future.

To Annabelle and Steven.

TOAST TO BRIDE AND GROOM

(Sincere speech by a friend on the occasion of a second or third marriage where both parties have been divorced or widowed at least once. Select part, or all, of the following paragraphs, according to whether the parties have been recently widowed/divorced or alone for many years.)

All marriages are special occasions but a second marriage is a doubly precious time because you do not take everything for granted. You realize how very lucky you are to be given another chance to be happy, and appreciate the blessing you have received in finding a soulmate and companion you can trust. It is a time of renewed hope.

I know that the two of you who are getting married today feel it is wonderful to be with so many good friends, and in particular one good friend, who understands your heartaches as well as your joys. That is so important.

It is a pleasure for you to experience an end to loneliness and sadness, and a joy for us to be witnesses and share this beginning with you. When you have experienced past disappointments, hardship and disillusionment, you know you have been up and down on life's waves. And when you are in the troughs of those waves, you sometimes wonder when you will ever come up again. Yet there is always a chance anew, an opportunity to feel love for someone, just like the first time. The past does not burden the present – but you learn by it, and do not repeat your mistakes. You have an opportunity through experience for knowing better than anyone else what is at stake and how much effort it takes, and what a loss it is if you don't do everything you can to make your partner contented. How fortunate you are to have found yet another chance at happiness together, with a better understanding than most people of what you should do to make a successful marriage, and how much you will gain.

It is difficult late in life to put away the past, and start again, but you have all the means at your disposal to make a success of the venture. Everyone has the right to happiness, and should you have the chance to find happiness, whether you are someone young starting life again, or a grandmother, why not?

We are confident that you will now receive the joy you deserve, and we are really happy for you. I speak for everyone here when I say we wish you all the best, and hope that for you (pause) 'the best is yet to come'. So, Annabelle and Steven, we would like to drink a toast to your happy future together. (Raise glass.)

To Annabelle and Steven.

SPEECHES TO AVOID

Overapologetic speech
I don't know why anyone picked me to give a speech. I've never given a speech in my life before. And I'm sure you don't want a long speech but I've tried to prepare something, and I hope it's all right. Anyway, all I can say is, I did make some notes somewhere, I think I put them in my pocket, or maybe (silence). Well, I can't find them, but (pause), oh, here it is. I've got a joke! 'As I was on my way to the wedding' (pause). Oh, I've dropped it! Can you move your chair? No, don't bother. It's not really funny, and you've probably heard it anyway. Most of you don't know Alf, but I expect you'll want to wish him, and the bride of course, a happy, er, future.

Negative speech – and rather too revealing!
I don't like speeches and I didn't want to give a speech, but Martha insisted I should. I suppose there was nobody else. I'm not a good speaker so I'm not going to bore you by making a long speech.

Anne's a nice girl. I went out with Anne for a long time before she decided to marry Alfred, or he decided to marry her. So I suppose it's what she wanted and she's done the right thing. Anyway, they know each other pretty well, having been living together for two years now. They wouldn't have got married if she hadn't been pregnant, so the baby has done something good. I know her Mum's pleased. The baby's going to be a big change. Everyone says, 'May all your troubles be little ones'. Apart from that I don't suppose they'll have any troubles. Marriage won't be a big change for them as they'll be living in the same place, you know. So everything is going to be all right, more or less.

Er – what else am I supposed to say? If you haven't got a drink the bar's still open. Prices are a bit steep but you don't go to weddings every day. We're going to pass the hat round later, buy some beer and go back to their place. Anne's shaking her head. What's the matter? Don't you want us to? Alfred says it's all right. Anyway, if you can't afford the whisky and you haven't got any beer left, grab a glass of water. To Anne and Alf! Can I sit down now?

Extremely brief reply from the bridegroom
Thank you.

Depressing speech
Relatives and friends, the one person missing here today is of course, Anne's father, and no day can be really happy without him with us. Though I have tried to take his place, it is mere formality. No-one can take his place. Our happiness would have been complete if he had been here. Alas he is not. We miss his help and his advice, as a husband to Martha, and father to Anne. He made so many plans for this wedding. If only he could have seen Anne today ... (breaks off). Has somebody got a handkerchief to give to Anne?'

Reluctant father-in-law's speech

We're very pleased to see Anne getting married, at last. When I first met Alfred I didn't like him very much, because of his hair and his clothes and the fact that he didn't have a steady job, but now I've got to know him he doesn't seem too bad. All these are things which can be changed. I'm sure Anne could change him if she wanted to, but she seems to like him the way he is. We're sorry that his Mum, what's her name?, died, and that his Dad didn't come along with his new stepmother, but perhaps it's just as well. Anyway, um, where was I? Well, er, I think that's everything. Let's all have a drink. Was I supposed to toast somebody?

Gushing speech

I am deeply honoured to be invited to this momentous and lavish occasion by my esteemed friends, Martha and George. It is a privilege to pay them this small token of respect. I am sure Martha will forgive me for saying that her very presence excites envy from others. Martha has always been admired for her brilliant elegance, the epitome of good taste. The evidence before our eyes is her faultless attention to detail in these exquisite flower decorations. It has been a day which commenced so stunningly with the horse and carriage procession, swept forward with the harmonious, soaring, musical arrangements at the wedding ceremony, and has culminated in the utter perfection of the gourmet dinner, all in keeping with what we have come to expect from the organizational abilities of one of the world's paragons. No woman on earth could have been a more devoted, exacting, wife and mother, and Annabelle has admirably followed her mother's fine example, having inherited flawless cover-girl looks, and demonstrating impeccable good manners. You will, I am quite sure, agree with me totally when I say, our beautiful, delectable, Annabelle is irreplacable, and we shall miss her dreadfully, when she departs across the skies to the beautiful tropical paradise which she will enhance immeasurably ...

Long pompous speech

Your Royal Highness, ladies and gentlemen, as a minister, judge and professor, I feel I am in a good position to speak about the history of marriage, its importance in society, and the duties of the married couple to each other and the wider community. First, the history of marriage (continues) ...

Now, we shall continue with the sayings of the numerous venerable sages (continues) ...

... Well, I agreed not to speak more than half an hour, but I see that I have been speaking for a little longer than forty-five minutes. I could continue considerably longer on this fascinating subject, in fact I have several pages of notes here if anybody wishes to come and ask me any questions. Unfortunately I am obliged to terminate at this stage, because someone has just passed me a note saying that the band has to depart at 11 pm, and it is now 10.30. So I will conclude by saying that (continues) ...

JOKES, COMIC STORIES & ANECDOTES

On a happy occasion such as a wedding, jokes and comic stories are welcome and make a particularly good ending for a speech. If you cannot tell long jokes without getting lost, stick to one-liners. Try out each of your jokes on someone who will not be at the wedding to see if it sounds funny the way you tell it.

FINDING A JOKE

Books of quotations and joke books provide sources. Humorous books related to your subjects are also useful.

Turn for advice to witty friends, those who are often invited to give speeches, or to professional speech writers. When constructing a funny story remember that one of the elements of humour in the punchline is surprise, going suddenly from the sublime to the ridiculous, from exhilaration to despair, from discovery of a tragedy to self-centred concern about some minor problem.

CHANGING CLICHES

Two dangers with cliches such as 'May all their troubles be little ones' are that older members of the audience have heard them before and that the previous speaker may use the same joke or saying. To create a more original effect well-known phrases and sayings can be contrasted with others which contradict them. To be sure of surprise and originality adapt the joke to a new locality or profession, or better still find a funny story based on a situation taken from real life.

AVOIDING UNSUITABLE SUBJECT MATTER

The Victorians said that at the dinner table you should not discuss sex, politics or religion. Similarly in a wedding speech statements about religion or politics might result in a quarrel or give offence by causing people with opposing views to disagree, insult each other, or try to convert each other. Sexual references might give offence, as can double entendres. As a general rule you should avoid unintentionally offending friends or potential friends, but instead flatter or compliment them.

If your audience is Irish, even if you are Irish, you do not want a joke which makes Irish people appear stupid, but clever instead. The same applies to Jews or any other national or religious group. Remember, that unless you have inspected the wedding list and know everybody on both sides of the family you can never be sure who is in a large audience.

ADAPTING JOKES

Jokes have a vogue. The same jokes are told about foreigners in different countries. The jokes told about the Irish in England are told about the Belgians in France. They are really stock jokes, and often have little reference to the nationalities mentioned.

If the most amusing anecdote you can find is one which is rather negative, tell it and then disassociate yourself from the views it expresses. For example, supposing you want to refer to the fact that the groom is a medical student and you have a story about a king dying in the Middle Ages who says the physician has killed him, tell this story but end it, 'Of course medicine has come a long way since those days'.

Another way to tell a joke without directing it against your subject is to refer it to other people. For example, if you wanted to use the line that, 'Doctors bury their mistakes' without appearing to criticize the bridegroom who is a medical student or doctor, you could say that 'other doctors' bury their mistakes.

In addition to deleting anything in bad or questionable taste, you might like to add a national, regional or personal dimension to a good joke. Jokes can become more amusing if you can perfect the appropriate accent, or introduce local placenames and references. So if you find a good Irish joke and want to tell it about another local or ethnic group you could do so. To perfect the accent you could obtain one of many BBC records of stories told in various accents. Alternatively if you are trying to use an accent because some members of the wedding party speak like that, get one of them to record a short passage for you on tape and play it over until you have perfected their accent.

A SHORT COMPENDIUM OF JOKE THEMES

Actors

I come not to bury Caesar but to praise (bridegroom's name). When an accomplished actor like (bridegroom's name) realizes he is going to have a speaking part in the wedding ceremony he jumps at the opportunity. Alas, being the best man at an actor's wedding is like trying to direct an actor who wants to direct. At the wedding rehearsal we got the video camera out and (bridegroom's name) said, 'To do or not to do ...' Then he asked who was the understudy.

As an actor myself, I wanted a part, too, but there isn't a speaking part for the best man at a wedding ceremony. So (bridegroom's name) very kindly invited me to give a speech. I was a trifle nervous when I remembered all the films I'd seen about weddings. There's Jane Eyre where the wedding is interrupted by someone who says the groom is already married. When we did the rehearsal again and Steven got it right I asked myself, has he played this scene before? Worse still, on the day, how could I be sure, with so many actors around, that the bridesmaids wouldn't turn out to be actors in drag? You can imagine my relief now that it's all over, and that it has turned out to be such a beautiful, conventional, dream wedding. They played their parts perfectly.

Builders/Decorators
It is harder to build than to destroy.

Cinema/Theatre/Wedding Ushers/Usherettes
A woman in the audience/church left in the middle of the performance/wedding and as she left she trod on the foot of the man at the end of the row. When she returned she said, 'Did I tread on your foot on the way out?'

'Yes, he replied.'

'Good!' she said, 'Then this is my row.'

Committees/Office Workers
A camel is a horse which got designed by a committee.

Computer Operators
President Kennedy said to an astronaut, 'Man is still the most extraordinary computer of all.'

To err is human. To really foul things up requires a computer.

Always check computerized bills. When we had just married our only gas consumption was the cooker, but we had a bill which would have enabled us to have cooked meals for the whole of Harrow.

Craftsperson
I asked (bride's/bridesgroom's name) what he/she did and he/she said, 'I'm a craftsperson.'

'Ah, I said, crafty, eh?'

Cricket
Foreigners often ask me to explain the rules of cricket. A cricket game lasts up to five days. There are eleven

players in each team. We do not follow the decimal system. That's 'not cricket'. We do not follow the British system of counting in dozens. That is not cricket. We count in elevens. That is cricket. Three important words are in and out and over. In cricket there is a wicket. One man stands near the wicket and bats and another bowls. The batsman is in. If he knocks down the wicket with his own leg, he is out. If he hits the ball he runs. There's another batsman who runs too, in the opposite direction. Every six balls they change the bowler. That's called an over. But the game isn't over. Not until they're all out. That's not the end of the game either, just the end of that innings. Now you know all the ins and outs of cricket. Simple, isn't it!

Dancing
We had to ask the bridesmaids not to pirouette in the aisle.

The bride was going to get married in a tutu but we persuaded her against it.

Dentists/Dental Technicians
What makes you nervous about them is that when you go to dinner with them, they pump up the chair.

Doctors/Nurses/Medical
In the dress rehearsal when she held out her finger for the ring he took her pulse./In the dress rehearsal when he held out the ring to her she took his pulse.

We have three empty seats today. One of these was for a doctor who has gone to the Middlesex Hospital. The other seats were for a couple who didn't know their way to this hall and decided to follow *his* car. We just had a call from them. They're at the Middlesex Hospital. They want to know the way back.

Most doctors have three things on their mind, ill, pill and bill. But he's/she's such a successful doctor he/she can afford to tell the patients when there's nothing wrong with them.

Good doctors aim to add life to your years, not just years to your life.

Drinking a Toast

A glass of wine/whisky/champagne is said to cure all sorts of ills such as the common cold. All you need is a candle and a glass of wine/whisky/champagne. Light the candle, drink the first glass and wait five minutes. Drink another glass and wait, still watching the candle. Keep drinking until you see three candles, then snuff out the middle one and go to sleep.

Drivers (of buses, taxis, cars, lorries)

The French chauffeurs/Israeli motorists/Glasgow/Dublin drivers/East End taxi drivers/bus drivers, like (bridegroom's name) and his Dad are skilful, safe drivers. I was in a car/taxi/bus once which shot through a red light. At the next crossing it shot through another red light. The third light was green and it skidded to a halt. 'Why did you do that?' I asked.

He (bridegroom's name) said, 'You can't be too careful. There could have been another car/coach/taxi coming the other way!'

Farmers and Footballers

Football coach, Bear Bryant, is also a farmhand and in the old days farmhands used to guide a team of animals in front of the plough, encouraging them and making sure they all pulled together. But he also coaches a football team and his secret for teamwork is this. What he says is that if anything goes badly, he tells the team, 'I did it'. If anything goes reasonably well, he says, 'We did it!' But when everything goes really well, he says to them, 'You did it!' Marriage is not a game: it is a team.

Finance

Charles Dickens had some advice on budgeting. The character Mr Micawber was based on Dickens' father and according to Dickens, Mr Micawber said, 'Annual income twenty pounds, annual expenditure nineteen and sixpence, result happiness. Annual income twenty pounds, annual expenditure twenty pounds and sixpence, result misery.' (Pause.) Mr Micawber's problem was he didn't have an account at (name bride's or bridegroom's bank/business).

Jane Austen said, 'It is a truth universally acknowledged, that a single man in possession of a good fortune must be in want of a wife.' She must have been thinking of Steven (bridegroom's name). However, she must also have been thinking of Annabelle (bride's name) when she added, 'She was of course only too good for him: but as nobody minds what is too good for them, he was very steadily earnest in pursuit of the blessing.'

Food Industry Worker/Waiters/Waitresses

It is said that Colman's Mustard made their money from the amount of mustard left on the plate.

A customer asked (bridegroom's name) if the fruit salad was fresh. 'Yes,' he said, 'fresh last week!'

A diner called over Annabelle/Steven and said, 'Waiter, waiter .../Waitress, waitress, there's a ...'

Golfers

Golf has been defined as a good walk spoilt.

All is fair in love and golf.

One thing you should remember: when he says, 'I just made a hole in one,' don't say, 'I didn't see you. Do it again, dear'.

You've all heard of golf widows. Golfers have all sorts of excuses about why they get home late. There was one who told his wife, 'The reason I'm late is that Harry died at the third hole, so we had to go all the way round the other fifteen holes on the course, dragging Harry.'

Gardeners/Grocers/Greengrocers
George has the best fruit/fruit trees. One day a little boy was standing looking at his apples/apple trees. George (name of bridegroom, father-in-law) said, 'Were you trying to take an apple?'

The little boy answered, 'No. I was trying not to take an apple.'

Greek Language Lesson
Steven's (groom's name) language is Greek and the Greek alphabet may be all Greek to you but it is surprising how much Greek we all use. A popular Greek saying is 'Know Thyself', which dates back to the ancient Greeks. Everybody has heard of Socrates and Plato. At college we did a philosophy course and we were very impressed to see a student reading Plato in the original Greek. Then we discovered the student was Greek! (Bridegroom's name) explained to me the Greek alphabet which is really very familiar. It goes from alpha to omega, beginning Alpha, beta, gamma, delta. From these we get our word alphabet, delta, and gamma which gives us gamma rays. And iota means very little. I asked (bridegroom's name) what the Greek for 'I' is. 'Ego' is I. Everybody here has an ego. You can tell that (bridegroom's name) is a good teacher. He makes it all sound so easy.

Journalists/Printers/Newsagents
A journalist is someone who hears shouts from a river, rushes up and asks, 'Are you all right?' When the man shouts back, 'I'm drowning,' the journalist replies, 'You're out of luck. You've missed the evening edition. But we can give you a paragraph in the morning edition.'

Adapt this by inserting bride's or groom's name; e.g. 'When Steven/Annabelle was a young reporter he/she heard a shout from someone drowning in a river ...'

A journalist tries to get into places other people are trying to get out of.

Some journalists work for the paper read by the people who run the country (The Times). Some journalists work for the paper read by the people who think they run the country (The Telegraph). Some journalists work for the paper read by the people who want to run the country (The Mail/The Express). Some journalists work for the paper whose readers don't care who runs the country so long as the girl on page three is well endowed (The Sun). And some journalists work for the paper read by the people who think this country should be run by another country (The Morning Star).

(Adapt this by finishing with appropriate newspaper or magazine e.g. 'But (bridegroom's name) works for the paper read by the people who want to buy a Ford Granada for fourpence/by twenty stone women who want to be as slim as Twiggy by Tuesday/Saturday (day of wedding)' etc. This can be equally adapted to American or other foreign newspapers).

Lawyers, Judges, and Solicitors
A jury consists of twelve persons chosen to decide who has the better lawyer.

(Robert Frost)

Managers
The secret of good management is, never put off until tomorrow what you can get someone else to do today, especially if you want it done yesterday.

Musicians/Singers
As a keen musician and clarinet player (name your own musical instrument or say 'As one who appreciates music but cannot play anything more difficult than a gramophone record, I was very impressed to learn) I was delighted to learn that Annabelle's uncle plays for the BBC orchestra (or pop group, etc.), on the violin (or drums). He has played us excerpts from Wagner's Ring Cycle. We managed to persuade him not to perform the whole work during the wedding ceremony.

Philosophy Teachers
A philosopher is a man who, when you ask how his wife is, replies, 'In relation to whom?'

Politics
Politics is not a bad profession. If you succeed there are many rewards. If you disgrace yourself you can always write a book. *(Ronald Reagan)*

Post Office Workers
They deliver letters everywhere, even the cemetery – Dead Letters.

Psychiatrists and Psychologists
I am often asked the difference between a psychologist and a psychiatrist. I say that a psychologist deals with the things normal people say and do, while a psychiatrist deals with the things dotty people say and do. When two psychologists are in a lift and a man gets into the lift and says hello, one psychologist turns to another and asks, 'What do you think he meant by that?'

Second Marriages
I'm not so old, and not so plain,
And I'm quite prepared to marry again.

(W. S. Gilbert)

Shopkeepers
The following type of story might be told by the best
man, a friend, or groom who works in the bride's family
business:

Annabelle's family have owned their furniture shop for
over 100 years and it is easy to see why they are a success
if you have had the privilege of actually working for
them, as I have. When customers buy on sunny days and
then change their minds when the goods are delivered
the next day, a rainy day, goods are returned frequently
in wet plastic sheets. Annabelle's father insists that any
furniture order is delivered the same day, even if it means
driving fifty miles and doing the driving and shifting
himself. That means the customer gets the goods while
still enthusiastic – and is very satisfied.

Social Workers/Prison Visitors
When Pope John XXIII visited prison he said to the inmates 'You could not come to see me so I have come to see you.'

Steven/Annabelle went to visit a woman in prison who was accused of poisoning a relative/colleague. Now it isn't easy to deal with this sort of situation. But Annabelle/Steven won the woman's confidence. The woman showed her appreciation by baking Annabelle/Steven a cake.

Sport
Wellington said that the Battle of Waterloo was won on the playing fields of Eton.

Statisticians
Everybody asks me what a statistician does. This story will explain it. A treasury statistician came down the steps of the ministry and met a beggar who held out his hand and said, 'Spare a shilling, mister? I haven't eaten for a week!'

The statistician replied, 'Really? And how does that compare with the same period last year?'

Teachers
One of the most difficult tasks of a teacher is to tell a father that his son can't cope with the new maths. But you can soften the blow by telling his Dad that none of the other dads can do it either.

Television
Buckminster Fuller said television is the third parent.

On television, detective series end at just the right moment, after the criminal has been caught and before the courts turn him loose.

Tennis Players

Annabelle (bride's name) and Steven (groom's name) are both tennis players – the perfect match.

Vets/Pet Lovers

Vets have very strange conversations on the phone. Sometimes we are on call at someone else's house, and a call is referred from a dog-owner and a relative hears us saying, 'And how is his third leg?'

In America the pet department at Macy's stocks dresses and bows for the best-dressed poodle. We did think of bringing a pooch along to follow the bride, dressed as a bridesmaid.

Other sources of ideas can be found in the books of the well-known author-vet James Herriot and humorous poems on cats and dogs can be found in the collected works of T. S. Eliot.

Wedding Customs

The French have some amusing wedding customs. When the dance music starts they play games. The first time the music stops every man gives his right shoe to his partner. Then he turns and dances with the woman behind. Next time the music stops he gives away his left shoe and again takes the partner behind. Then the woman gives away her right shoe, then her left shoe, then the man removes his jacket, then his tie. After the music stops for the last time the first man to return the ladies' shoes and collect up all his clothing is allowed to kiss every woman in the room!

Work

Some people like to rest. 'I like work. I can enjoy watching it for hours.' Others are workaholics who cannot stop working. Pius XII said to doctors who told him to cut down on his work schedule, 'I shall be able to rest one minute after I die.'

Of every 100 people in this country 55 per cent are of working age. At any one time fifteen per cent are unemployed, that leaves 40 per cent. Of these, five per cent are sick, leaving 35 per cent. Of these, five per cent are on strike, leaving 30 per cent. At this time of year 20 per cent are on holiday, leaving 10 per cent. And of these, 8 per cent are looking after children or relatives. That leaves you and me. That means all the work has to be done by Annabelle (bride's name) and me (groom's name).

One hundred people said they would help Matilda (insert bride's mother's name) organize the wedding. Of these fifty-five were at work. Five were looking for work. Five were away on business. One was minding the shop/on night duty/taking exams. (Continue as above.) That left only Annabelle and me to help with the washing up. But we are going away on our honeymoon. Now you appreciate how much work and effort and thought Matilda (bride's mother's name) has put into organizing this wonderful wedding.

Writers
When Agatha Christie was asked where she got her plots she replied, 'Harrods'.

ANECDOTES
Other humorous and serious anecdotes can be obtained by speaking to the subjects of your speech or their families and colleagues. Ask them: What was the most surprising thing that happened to you when you started working on the buses/in the shop/in the hospital/in the school? Have there been any funny customers/patients/pupils/incidents? Who was your

best pupil/patient? What was the most useful thing you learnt when you started working/teaching? Did you have any disasters at the beginning? What was your greatest success?

There are many ready-made collections of anecdotes available in book form. Try browsing along the reference shelves of your local library, or the humour section of the local bookshop.

QUOTATIONS

Add spice to your speech and toast by inserting an amusing, interesting or relevant quotation. This chapter includes a selection of quotations for the most common subjects you are likely to want to cover: love, marriage, weddings, family, work and hobbies and so on. Libraries and bookshops stock treasuries of quotations.

OCCUPATIONAL HEROES AND HAZARDS

If the bride's or groom's family is in the entertainment professions it is easy to produce a humorous quotation from an actor, singer, movie star, television personality, songwriter, or playwright. These suit numerous ancillary professions, such as TV company employees, where the fun can be enjoyed by rival organizations. Statesmen and politicians in the family offer equally numerous opportunities for choosing quotations from famous world leaders.

For relevant quotations for other occupations, look in trade journals and magazines.

RELIGIOUS AND INSPIRATIONAL SUBJECTS

For locating religious quotations, concordances to the Bible will direct you to quotations in the Old and New Testament. Many religious organizations keep stocks of books in their bookshops or libraries. If you are getting married at a particular church or synagogue you may be granted access to a library not normally opened to the public. The priest, minister, rabbi, or other community leader probably knows sources and will most likely quote them to you from memory if you telephone or approach him or her after a service. If you cannot find help from the nearest religious Catholic, Protestant, Methodist, Hindu, Moslem, Buddhist, or Jewish organization, try the history or language departments of colleges – Hebrew Studies, Arabic Studies, Modern Languages for French and Spanish Language & Literature, Oriental Studies, or Asian Languages.

WITTY QUOTATIONS

Well-known humorous writers include James Thurber, Charles Dickens, Mark Twain, Jane Austen, Oscar Wilde, George Bernard Shaw and of course William Shakespeare. There are concordances to Shakespeare and a *Who's Who In Dickens*.

Songwriters are another good source of quotable lines. You can track down the words of songwriters from books of librettos, record sleeves, or by playing their records or cassettes if you have a lot of time to spare. Try W. S. Gilbert, Sammy Cahn, and Noel Coward or a dictionary of popular music

AMERICAN AND CANADIAN QUOTATIONS

American quotations can be found among the sayings of every past President from Washington, Jefferson, Lincoln, Roosevelt, and Kennedy to Reagan. Politics, business, morality, and determination to win against the odds are popular subjects. *The Oxford Companion to American Literature* will help to locate American novels, plays and other books.

Depending on the language spoken and preferred by Canadians in your audience, you can quote from either English or French authors, or both, as well as modern Canadian authors, or traditional favourites such as L. M. Montgomery who wrote the ever-popular *Anne of Green Gables* and Mazo de la Roche who wrote the *Jalna* series.

FINDING POEMS

Unless you are a great actor or orator avoid any verse over four lines long. Five-line limericks, however, add humour, but be sure they are in good taste. Your local library should have poetry anthologies for your reference.

ADAPTING QUOTATIONS

The more you can relate your quotations to your audience and the people you are praising in your speech, the more interested and flattered they will feel. If the only quotation you can find is not very relevant or complimentary, adapt it. For example, when the subject of your speech is a soldier you could start, 'According to the British Grenadiers, "Some talk of Alexander, and some of Hercules, and others of Lysander and such great names as these." But I would rather talk about Captain (bridegroom's name).'

A SELECTION OF QUOTATIONS

To make the following quotations more suitable for delivery in a speech I have updated those using old-fashioned language.

Quotations
It is a good thing for an uneducated man to read books of quotations.

(Winston Churchill)

Actors
Actors are never out of work. They are always resting.
(See Telegrams below.)

Acting and Law
The law and the stage – both are a form of exhibition.
(Orson Welles)

Advertising
A picture is worth a thousand words.

Half the money spent on advertising is wasted, but we don't know which half.

Advice
In giving advice I advise you, be short.

(Horace)

Don't give a woman advice; one should never give a woman anything she can't wear in the evening.

(Oscar Wilde)

When angry, count to a hundred.

(Mark Twain)

Tact is the art of making a point without making an enemy. The most difficult thing in the world is to know how to do a thing and to watch someone else doing it wrong and keep quiet.

Live within your means, even if you have to borrow money to do it.

God helps them that help themselves.

(Benjamin Franklin)

Happy the man, and happy he alone,
He who can call today his own:
He who, secure within, can say,
Tomorrow do thy worst, for I have lived today.

(Dryden)

Look before you leap,
For as you sow, you're likely to reap.

(Samuel Butler)

To err is human: to forgive, divine.
Education forms the common mind:
Just as the twig is bent, the tree's inclined.

(Alexander Pope)

If you can fill the unforgiving minute
With sixty seconds' worth of distance run
Yours is the earth and everything that's in it,
And – which is more – you'll be a man, my son.
(Rudyard Kipling)

Be thou familiar, but by no means vulgar....
Costly thy habit as thy purse can buy.
But not expressed in fancy; rich, not gaudy,
For the apparel oft proclaims the man.
Neither a borrower or a lender be;
For oft the loan loses both itself and friend,
And borrowing dulls the edge of husbandry
This above all: to thine own self be true,
And it must follow, as the night the day,
Thou canst not then be false to any man.
Farewell; my blessing season this in thee.
(William Shakespeare
– Polonius' speech to Laertes in Hamlet)

Forgive one another, as God forgives you.
(New Testament)

No act of kindness, no matter how small, is ever wasted.
(Aesop)

To be prepared is half the victory.
(Miguel de Cervantes)

A place for everything and everything in its place.
(Samuel Smiles)

Don't put it down, put it away.

(Popular Maxim)

Age
Age brings wisdom. American millionaire, Bernard

Baruch, said that, 'an elder statesman is somebody old enough to know his mind – and keep quiet about it'.

You're only young once, and if you work it right, once is enough.

(Joe E. Lewis)

Wrinkles should merely indicate where smiles have been.
(Mark Twain)

Grow old along with me!
The best is yet to be.

(Robert Browning)

Time still, as he flies, adds increase to her truth,
And gives to her mind what he steals from her
    youth.

(Edward Moore)

Bachelor
He could have made many women happy by remaining a bachelor. He could also have made one woman happy by remaining a bachelor.

(Adapted)

Advice to those about to marry. Don't!

(Punch, 1845)

When a lady's in the case,
You know, all other things give place.

(John Gay)

Oh! how many torments lie in the small circle of a wedding ring!

(Colley Cibber)

A man is so in the way in the house.　　*(Mrs Gaskell)*

His designs were strictly honourable, as the phrase is; that is, to rob a lady of her fortune by way of marriage.

(Henry Fielding)

Beauty
Beauty is in the eye of the beholder.

Blessings, Thanks, Prayers and Hopes
The Lord is my shepherd; I shall not want....
Surely goodness and mercy shall follow me all the days of my life.

(Psalm 23. A Psalm of David)

God bless us and cause his face to shine upon us.

(Psalm 67)

Business
The business of America is business.

(President Calvin Coolidge)

There's no business like show business.

(Song)

Children
The little one lies in its cradle
The little one sits in its chair
And the light of heaven above
Transfigures its golden hair.

(Adapted from The Changeling *by James Russell Lowell)*

Children are your heritage, like arrows in the hand of a mighty man. Happy is the man who has his quiver full of them.

(Adapted from Psalm 127)

May your wife be like a fruitful vine growing by the side of your house, and your children like olive plants round about your table.

(Adapted from Psalm 128)

Drinking and Toasts
We'll drink a cup of kindness yet, for the sake of old lang's syne.

(Adapted from Robert Burns)

Drink to me only with thine eyes,
And I will pledge with mine;
Or leave a kiss within the cup,
And I'll not look for wine.

(Ben Jonson)

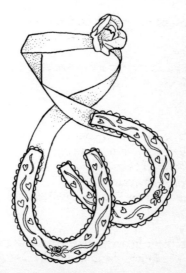

Engagements and Bachelor Parties

A man's friendships are, like his will, invalidated by marriage – but they are also no less invalidated by the marriage of his friends.

(*Samuel Butler*)

Families

Important families are like potatoes. The best parts are underground.

He that hath a wife and children hath given hostages to fortune.

(*Francis Bacon*)

The apple does not fall far from the tree.

(*Proverb*)

Everyone is the son of his own works.

(Don Quixote, *Miguel de Cervantes*)

The child is the father of the man.

(*William Wordsworth*)

Winston Churchill said, a family starts 'with a young man falling in love with a girl. No superior alternative has been found.'

A man must first govern himself ere he is fit to govern a family.

(*Sir Walter Raleigh*)

Father

A father of the fatherless is God.

(*Psalm 68*)

Honour thy father and thy mother.

(*Old Testament*)

Friendship
No man is useless while he has a friend.
(Robert Louis Stevenson)

One man in a thousand, Solomon says,
Will stick more close than a brother.
But the thousandth Man will stand by your side
To the gallows-foot – and after!
(Rudyard Kipling)

A faithful friend is the medicine of life.
(Ecclesiasticus)

Happiness consists not in the multitude of friends but in
their worth and choice. *(Ben Jonson)*

(The only way) to have a friend is to be one.
(Ralph Waldo Emerson)

Gardens
God the first garden made.
(Abraham Cowley)

One is nearer God's Heart in a garden
Than anywhere else on earth.
(Dorothy Gurney)

Our England is a garden, and such gardens are not
    made
By singing:—'Oh, how beautiful!' and sitting in the
    shade. *(Rudyard Kipling)*

Guests
Too late I stayed, – forgive the crime;
Unheeded flew the hours.
How noiseless falls the foot of time,
That only treads on flowers!
(Hon. William Robert Spencer)

Laugh and be merry together, like brothers akin,
Guesting awhile in the room of a beautiful inn.
Glad till the dancing stops, and the lilt of the music
    ends.
Laugh till the game is played; and be you merry my
    friends.
       (John Masefield – from Laugh and be Merry*)*

Handwriting
Like the lesser rivers on maps.
                  (Dorothy Parker)

Happiness
The greatest happiness of the greatest number.
                  (Jeremy Bentham)

Health and Wealth
If you enjoy good health, you are rich.

Early to bed and early to rise makes a man healthy,
wealthy and wise.

I wish you health; I wish you wealth; I wish you gold in
store; I wish you heaven when you die; what could I wish
you more?

Home and Away
East, west, home's best.

There is no place like home after the other places close.

    If solid happiness we prize,
    Within our breast this jewel lies;
    And they are fools who roam;

The world has nothing to bestow;
From our own selves our joys must flow,
And that dear place – our home.

(Nathaniel Cotton)

Wherever I roam, whatever realms I see,
My heart untravelled fondly turns to thee.

(Oliver Goldsmith)

't is distance lends enchantment to the view,
And robes the mountain in its azure hue.

(Thomas Campbell)

Honeymoon

Ten years ago the moon was source of inspiration for
lovers. In ten years time it will be just another airport.

(Emmanuel G. Mesthene – adapted)

House

I often wish that I had clear,
For life, six hundred pounds a year,
A handsome house to lodge a friend,
A river at my garden's end.

(Jonathan Swift)

Husbands

American women expect to find in their husbands a
perfection that English women only hope to find in their
butlers.

Being a husband is a whole time job.

(Arnold Bennett)

Husbands love your wives and do not be bitter against
them.

(New Testament, Colossians)

Jealousy

First, then, a woman will, or won't, – depend on it;
If she will do it, she will; and there's the end of it.
But if she won't, since safe and sound your trust is,
Fear is affront: and jealousy injustice.

(Aaron Hill)

Law

Good laws make it easier to do right and harder to do wrong.

(William Gladstone)

I was never ruined but twice, once when I lost a lawsuit and once when I won one.

(Voltaire)

Love

Whatever you do . . . love those who love you.

(Voltaire)

Love and marriage go together like a horse and carriage.

(Sammy Cahn – song)

Whoever loved that loved not at first sight?

(Christopher Marlowe)

And to his eye
There was but one beloved face on earth
And that was shining on him.

(Lord Byron)

A thing of beauty is a joy forever.

(John Keats)

Love conquers all.

(Virgil)

None but the brave deserve the fair.

(Dryden)

He will hold thee, when his passion shall have spent
    its novel force,
Something better than his dog, a little dearer than
    his horse.

(Alfred Lord Tennyson)

The meeting of two personalities is like the contact of
two chemical substances; if there is any reaction, both
are transformed.

(Carl Jung)

The course of true love never did run smooth.

(William Shakespeare)

Love does not consist in gazing at each other, but in
looking outward in the same direction.

(Antoine de Saint-Exupery)

Marriage
Here's to marriage, that happy estate that resembles a
pair of scissors: 'So joined that they cannot be separated,
often moving in opposite directions, yet punishing
anyone who comes between them.'

(Sydney Smith)

Marriage is a bargain and somebody has to get the worst
of a bargain.

(Helen Rowland)

Let me not to the marriage of true minds
Admit impediments.

(William Shakespeare)

It is a woman's business to get married as soon as possible and a man's to keep unmarried as long as he can.

(George Bernard Shaw)

Marriage is popular because it combines the maximum of temptation with the maximum of opportunity.

(George Bernard Shaw)

Marriage is like a cage; one sees the birds outside desperate to get in; and those inside desperate to get out.

(Montaigne)

Happiness in marriage is entirely a matter of chance.

(Jane Austen)

Second Marriage
To lose one husband is a misfortune. To lose two looks like carelessness.

(Jane Austen)

The triumph of hope over experience.

(Dr Samuel Johnson)

'Tis better to have loved and lost than never to have loved at all.

(Alfred Lord Tennyson)

We're number two. We try harder.

(Avis Car Rental advertisement)

When I lost my wife every family in town offered me another.

(Proverb)

I chose my wife, as she did her wedding gown, for qualities that would wear well.

(Oliver Goldsmith)

When widows exclaim loudly against second marriages, I would always lay a wager, that the man, if not the wedding-day, is absolutely fixed on.

(Henry Fielding)

And on her lover's arm she leant,
And round her waist she felt it fold,
And far across the hills they went
In that new world which is the old.

(Alfred Lord Tennyson)

...speak of one that loved not wisely but too well; of one not easily jealous, but being wrong perplex'd in the extreme.

(William Shakespeare)

Medicine
The art of medicine consists of amusing the patient while nature cures the disease.

(Voltaire)

The bible according to St Mary's.

(Popular saying in London among hospital doctors, 1987)

Doctors bury their mistakes. *(Popular saying)*

I am dying from the treatment of too many physicians.

(Alexander the Great)

God heals and the doctor takes the fee.

(Benjamin Franklin)

Men and Character
The test of a man or woman's breeding is how they behave in a quarrel.

(George Bernard Shaw)

Men and Women
Men have sight, women insight.

(Victor Hugo)

Mining
O the collier lad, he's a canny lad.

(The Coal-filler's Song, *Johnny Handle*)

Money
Money is like a sixth sense without which you cannot make use of the other five.

(W. Somerset Maugham)

Get money; still get money, boy;
No matter by what means.

(Ben Jonson)

Mothers
A mother is a mother still,
The holiest thing alive.

(Samuel Taylor Coleridge)

For a wife take the daughter of a good mother.

(Thomas Fuller)

Lincoln said, All that I am, or hope to be, I owe to my angel mother.

A mother's love endures through all; in good repute, in bad repute, in the face of the world's condemnation, a mother still loves on, and still hopes that her child may turn from his evil ways, and repent; she ... remembers the infant smiles ... the joyful shout of childhood, and the ... promise of his youth; and she can never be brought to think him all unworthy.

(Washington Irving)

The hand that rocks the cradle ... rules the world.
(William Ross Wallace)

Motoring
In a Rolls Royce the loudest noise is the ticking of the clock.

(Advertisement)

He was right, dead right, as he sped along,
But he's just as dead as if he were wrong.
(Humorous Epitaph)

Music
If music be the food of love, play on.
(William Shakespeare)

Music hath charms to soothe a savage breast.
(William Congreve)

Police
A policeman's lot is not a happy one.

(W. S. Gilbert)

Sailing and the Sea
I must go down to the seas again, to the lonely sea
and the sky,
And all I ask is a tall ship and a star to steer her by.
(John Masefield)

They that go down to the sea in ships, that do business in great waters, see the works of the Lord, and his wonder in the deep. For he commands, and raises the stormy wind, which lifts up the waves. Then they cry to the Lord in their trouble and he brings them out of their distress. He makes the storm calm, so that the waves are still. Then they are glad because they are quiet, and he brings them into their desired haven.
(Psalm 107)

Secretary
A secretary must think like a man, act like a lady, look like a girl – and work like a dog.

Soldiers
Some talk of Alexander, and some of Hercules
And others of Lysander, and such great names as these.
(The British Grenadiers, *anonymous*)

Speeches
It usually takes me more than three weeks to prepare a good impromptu speech.
(*Mark Twain*)

You'd scarcely expect one of my age
To speak in public on the stage
And if I chance to fall below
Socrates or Cicero
Don't view me with a critic's eye
But pass my imperfections by.
Large streams from little fountains flow
Tall oaks from little acorns grow.
(*David Everett – adapted*)

Teaching
History teaches us that history teaches us nothing

He who can does; He who cannot teaches.

To be good is noble, but to teach others how to be good is nobler, and less trouble.
(*Mark Twain*)

Telegrams
When an actor has money he doesn't send letters; he sends telegrams.
(*Anton Checkhov*)

Television
Television is the third parent.
(Buckminster Fuller)

Travel
I know where I'm going and I know who's going with me
(Anon)

Welcome and Friendship
This land is your land
(Woody Guthrie)

Will ye no come back again?
(Scottish)

Whither thou goest I will go.
(Book of Ruth, Old Testament)

Winter
Now is the winter of our discontent ...
(William Shakespeare)

Wives
Merry wives of Windsor.
(William Shakespeare)

Women
The great question which I have never been able to answer is, 'What does a woman want?'
(Freud)

If men knew what women really think, they'd be ten times more daring.
(Alphonse Karr)

It is assumed that the woman must wait, motionless,
until she is wooed. That is how the spider waits for the
fly.

(*George Bernard Shaw*)

First, then, a woman will, or won't, – depend on it;
If she will do it, she will; and there's the end of it.

(*Aaron Hill*)

HOW TO INTRODUCE QUOTATIONS AND ANECDOTES INTO YOUR SPEECH

A slightly cumbersome but straightforward method is to
begin, 'When I knew I was going to have to mention
sailing, because that is Peter's great interest, I thought I
would look up what great writers and poets of the past
have said about sailing. The poet John Masefield said,
"…"' If the quotation is a common one you could
acknowledge this fact but turn it into a plus, 'We all
know the lovely poem by John Masefield, which you can
never tire of hearing, (Pause) "I must go down to the seas
…"'

If you happen to know your bride or bridegroom's
tastes you could say, 'I would like to read you just the
first verse/first two lines/last two lines of one of one of
Sharon's favourite poems about the sea. It was written
by John Masefield, and the title is Sea Fever.'

You may prefer to follow this by a lesser known
quotation from another author. You could then relate
their interest in the sea to what the bride and groom will
have in common, 'I hope they will have many happy
voyages/sailing trips together,' and finally relate your
subject to the wider issue of marriage, 'and enjoy the
voyage of life together'.

The symbolism of the sea has often been used by
writers and speakers, but a similar ploy can be used
relating to other professions, hobbies and subjects
ranging from football to plane travel with original effect.

Make all your points positive ones. If your audience includes members who speak different languages or hold different religious views make sure that they can enjoy the quotations too and feel that you are addressing them as well as appreciate their point of view. For example, you might say, 'Whatever your religious background, you can appreciate the beautiful poetry of the psalms.'

ON THE DAY

IS THERE ANYBODY THERE?

Make sure you have your audience's attention from the moment you stand up. It is disconcerting to try to talk to a group of people who are clearly not listening. Stand up and wait for silence. If necessary, tap a glass for attention before starting to speak. A few well-aimed, well-considered words above the hubbub may well do the trick. The first paragraph of your speech after the preamble should be designed to hold everyone's attention.

It is also worth remembering that the way to hold someone's attention is to look at them. You lose their attention if you keep staring down at the papers in your hand. Look around at the whole audience, those at the front, the left, the right, and the back. When you raise your head and look at them they will be able to see you clearly too.

The sound of somebody's name attracts their attention. You will not want to reprove any children for talking during your speech. But if the pageboy William is talking, making noises, or turning paper napkins into darts, you could say, 'All the children have been as good as they could be, even little William!' This should momentarily distract William from whatever he is doing and raise a laugh from neighbouring tables.

YOUR PROPS

Your Speech or Speech Notes

Whether you have chosen to write out a full speech or to use comprehensive, ordered notes, there will be your main prop. Where should you keep them handily? Select a place where they are easy to reach, and keep them there all the time so that you do not have to hunt for them. Women have no difficulty – the handbag is the obvious choice. For men, if you are right-handed your right-hand outside pocket would be a good place; if you are left handed, your left-hand pocket. A rented suit will be collected from a hire firm on the day before the wedding so make yourself a checklist which includes, 'Put speech notes in jacket pocket. Notes are now in desk.' If you are nervous or accident-prone, give a second copy to the best man or chief bridesmaid to guard against loss.

Handwritten notes may be hard to read when you are flustered, inebriated or reading in a dim light. It is also particularly difficult to discover your place in a speech after you have been looking up at the audience. Get the notes typewritten using a new ribbon, or copy them out in black felt tip pen in large capital letters. Write out large headings so that if possible you just need to glance at the headings to remind you of what to say.

Flimsy paper will rattle if your hands are shaking, betraying your nerves to the audience, and possibly making sounds over the microphone or on tape. So use card. If your pockets are small you may have to use index cards. Your speech may run over several cards. You want to avoid getting them in the wrong order or dropping them, so number them in the top corner, and link them together with a tag.

A Glass of Wine

You need a glass of wine to raise at the end of your speech if you are going to propose a toast. You may also want to have a tumbler of alcohol to sip to relax beforehand. But don't get so tiddly that you keep hiccoughing, or giggle all the way through, especially at your own jokes before you reach the punchline. And don't get so drunk that you can't stand up and have to sit down in the middle or, worse still, cannot speak at all. A glass of water is an ideal prop.

Additional Props

Unless you are in the entertainment world you will find that dressing up in conventional wedding clothes is quite time-consuming. For the bride there is the challenge of walking and dancing in a full length dress, and perhaps not getting tangled in the microphone cable. For the ushers wearing grey morning suits, tails and bow ties, and dancing in them, is quite enough excitement, not to mention keeping track of where you left the top hat. You will not want to perform a dance on the table, or change twenty costumes for non-stop comedy routines. However, just one prop such a funny hat, or a quick joke about how to get a grey top hat to fit, using a spare outsize one which comes right down over your eyes, can make the speech unusual. This could be effective at a wedding where grey top hats are worn, or even funnier at an informal wedding as part of a speech showing why they decided NOT to have a formal wedding!

WHAT TO AVOID

The first essential is to be there. Don't disappear into the loo at the vital moment.

If you are prone to stammering or stuttering you may prefer not to speak, although if you are the bridegroom others will probably insist upon it. Winston Churchill became a famous speaker even though he stuttered, because what he said was so interesting, and he persisted in public speaking. King George VI stammered but everyone was so sympathetic that his first radio broadcast on Christmas Day in wartime established the popular tradition of the royal Christmas Day speech.

Decide whether drink will make the problem worse or better. Eliminate from your speech any words containing awkward letters or multiple syllables. Many people stammer or stutter because they are nervous; but with sufficient determination you can carry this off with aplomb and turn it to your advantage by laughing at yourself, 'I am so hap–p–p . . . I'll try that again. Hap . . . No, I'm not going to get it right. I'm going to keep on being hap hap happy for the rest of my life!'

Avoid distracting mannerisms such as jingling keys and coins in your pocket. These sounds will be magnified by the microphone. Don't keep coughing, sniffing, and saying er, um, or 'you know'. Don't twiddle your hair, pull your ears, scratch your face, nor rub your nose or chin. Don't clench your fists tensely, or get so enthusiastic about what you are saying that you wave your arms about and knock over the wine. You may not knock over the wine, but the person sitting next to you and other members of the audience won't listen to your words. Your dramatic gestures will certainly mesmerize them, but they will be staring apprehensively at the glass, or laughing hysterically waiting for it to fall!

In order to cover up a faux pas do not look disconcerted but look pleased and pretend that the action was deliberate. For example, if somebody in the distant kitchen drops a tray with a clatter in the middle of your speech you could say, 'Applause at the end please!'

If there is a minor mishap you can make a joke of it. List all the worse mishaps which could have happened. These include the best man losing the ring, or going to the wrong church, and the groom finding the wrong woman when he lifts the veil. At one wedding the bridegroom and best man were standing on the wrong place, with the best man prompting a tongue-tied groom in a stage whisper. After the ceremony they really did discover that the minister had married the bride to the best man!

When latecomers appear through doors which slam noisily behind them and creep across the room in front of you, do not try to continue by raising your voice while your audience turn to look at the newcomers. There is a danger that the newcomers will dodge about trying to find somewhere to sit, and then whisper apologies to those near them, while you and your audience lose track of what you were saying. Instead you should pause, welcome them, and direct them to their seats: 'Aunt Mathilda, take a seat at the table. We're so glad you could make it. You're just in time for the toast to Annabelle. I was telling everyone how Annabelle met Steven in Kenya when they were on a safari holiday and ...'

HOW TO AD LIB

You must be prepared to reply to an unexpected remark or joke by the previous speaker. You will probably find that this comes naturally and that you are happier and more confident than you thought you would be. But don't be overconfident about what others will understand when making off the cuff remarks to those you know well. Leave out obscure remarks, jargon, and private jokes, otherwise you'll have to keep explaining them to people all evening.

You may find that you are subject to some good-natured heckling from the audience. Think of two or three things that might be called out and invent some amusing replies. If several remarks are shouted at you, your replies will fit one of them. Nobody will remember what you did not say. You will get credit for the quick-thinking repartee of your one success.

The names of those attending the wedding are usually known in advance but if not you may be able to look at the seating plan or guest list on the day and make some joke about the names, picking out amusing surnames such as, 'In this room we have a Black but no White, two Browns, some Blues, and a Green, but no 'reds'. 'I'm glad to see that Annabelle's family includes several Golds, a lot of Silver, two Smiths, and a Cook. Steven's family, I'm afraid, has no Silver at all, but they are very practical. They have a lot of Smiths. And a Baker.'

First names and family names offer other possibilities, if there are several Johns, Josephs, Marias, Mohammeds, or Joneses, Cohens, Singhs, or Patels. 'Annabelle told me to look out for her brother John. But when I found John he knew nothing about car maintenance. He was a musician.' Name something connected with the first John's job or home area. You then continue by naming the professions, the towns of origin, or the streets where the other Johns live. End, 'She didn't tell me there were fifteen Johns/Joneses/Patels in the family.'

The clothes of those attending can also be referred to, especially if you can introduce them into a joke. You say that the chief character in your joke or story was wearing such and such a hat or pair of shoes. You progress slowly, gradually adding more details. The suspense and amusement increases as more and more people realize you are referring to the bride's father, or the bridegroom's mother, or the person sitting on your right. Lastly the audience laughs as the person being described realizes it.

If it still goes wrong on the day, never mind. You can console yourself with the thought that you did your best. Don't worry too much about giving a good speech. This is a happy occasion and people aren't going to mind. Your effort has not been wasted. From now on you will listen with increased appreciation to the speeches of others. And whether you made mistakes or did well, you will be able to do better next time. Even if you only get married once, there will be more speeches to give or hear, at the weddings of your friends or your children. So enjoy yourself on the day. I am sure you will. Good luck!

INDEX